The Letter to the Ephesians

OneBook.

DAILY-WEEKLY

The Letter to the Ephesians

Fredrick J. Long

Printed in the United States of America

Cover design by Strange Last Name
Page design by PerfecType, Nashville, Tennessee

Long, Fredrick J., 1966-
   The letter to the Ephesians / Fred Long. – Frankin, Tennessee : Seedbed Publishing, ©2017.

   x, 145 pages ; 21 cm. + 1 videodisc – (OneBook. Daily-weekly)

   ISBN 9781628244069 (paperback)
   ISBN 9781628244106 (DVD)
   ISBN 9781628244076 (Mobi)
   ISBN 9781628244083 (ePub)
   ISBN 9781628244106 (uPDF)

   1. Bible. Ephesians--Textbooks.   2. Bible. Ephesians--Study and teaching.   3. Bible. Ephesians--Commentaries.   I. Title. II. Series.

BS2695.55.L66 2017   227/.50071   2017931370

SEEDBED PUBLISHING
Franklin, Tennessee
Seedbed.com

CONTENTS

CONTENTS

CONTENTS

WELCOME TO THE ONEBOOK DAILY-WEEKLY

John Wesley, in a letter to one of his leaders, penned the following,

> O begin! Fix some part of every day for private exercises. You may acquire the taste which you have not: what is tedious at first, will afterwards be pleasant.
>
> Whether you like it or not, read and pray daily. It is for your life; there is no other way; else you will be a trifler all your days. . . . Do justice to your own soul; give it time and means to grow. Do not starve yourself any longer. Take up your cross and be a Christian altogether.

Rarely are our lives most shaped by our biggest ambitions and highest aspirations. Rather, our lives are most shaped, for better or for worse, by those small things we do every single day.

At Seedbed, our biggest ambition and highest aspiration is to resource the followers of Jesus to become lovers and doers of the Word of God every single day; to become people of One Book.

To that end, we have created the OneBook: Daily-Weekly. First, it's important to understand what this is not: warm and fuzzy sentimental devotions. If you engage the Daily-Weekly for any length of time, you will learn the Word of God. You will grow profoundly in your love for God, and you will become a passionate lover of people.

How does the Daily-Weekly work?

Daily. As the name implies, every day invites a short but substantive engagement with the Bible. Five days a week you will read a passage of Scripture followed by a short segment of teaching and closing with a question for reflection and self-examination. On the sixth day, you will review and reflect on the prior five days.

Weekly. Each week, on the seventh day, find a way to gather with at least one other person doing the study. Pursue the weekly guidance for gathering.

Share learning, insight, encouragement, and most important, how the Holy Spirit is working in your lives.

That's it. Depending on the length of the study, when the eight or twelve weeks are done, we will be ready with the next study. On an ongoing basis we will release new editions of the Daily-Weekly. Over time, those who pursue this course of learning will develop a rich library of Bible learning resources for the long haul.

OneBook Daily-Weekly will develop eight- and twelve-week studies that cover the entire Old and New Testaments. Seedbed will publish new studies regularly so that an ongoing supply of group lessons will be available. All titles will remain accessible, which means they can be used in any order that fits your needs or the needs of your group.

If you are looking for a substantive study to learn Scripture through a steadfast method, look no further.

WEEK ONE

Ephesians 1:1–14

God's Great Plan: A Holy People

INTRODUCTION

The apostle Paul had a vision for how God was accomplishing his purposes for the world through the gospel of his beloved Son. Paul constantly related the work of Christ to God's expressed goals for humanity as revealed in Scripture. Paul's Scripture was, of course, the Jewish Scriptures, the Old Testament. At the same time, Paul understood the relevancy of the gospel, that is, the implications it had for believers living in the world. At the core, we see in Ephesians Paul's combination of Jewish scriptural understandings of God and God's revelation of Christ with first-century political conceptions of right rule and the right to rule. Thus, Ephesians in many ways represents Paul's statement of God's political vision for the world, but only as understood through the lens (or the revelation) of Jesus as the crucified Messiah.

This wonderful vision is clearly set forth in the opening fourteen verses of Ephesians. After Paul introduced himself, identified the letter recipients, and offered initial greetings (1:1–2), he unleashed one large sentence spanning twelve verses (1:3–14) in the underlying Greek text. Our English translations struggle to break the thoughts into separate, sensible sentences for us. But, we must ask, Why would Paul begin a letter in this fashion, with such a long, exuberant sentence? Well, there are two good reasons.

First, Paul expressed lavish praise on God with a corresponding lavish rhetorical style. He used a manner of speaking that his audiences in Ephesus and the surrounding region would have appreciated, especially when it came to honoring and praising politicians, such as kings, military commanders, and most recently and importantly, the Roman emperors. So, Paul's opening sentence to the Ephesians, which praises God's gifts, graces, peace, and salvation, essentially compares God's plan of salvation in Christ to the contemporary practice of praising emperors as human gods for their gifts, graces, peace, and salvation! Paul's language here occupies the same playing field of god(s) and politics. Yet, for Paul, this was not an even playing field, since God has placed Christ "far above all rule and authority and power and dominion, and above every name that is named, not only in this age but also in the age to come" (1:21). Yet, we should pay attention to where, how, and why Paul shows God in Christ surpassing all other religious and political claims.

Second, Paul's long sentence in 1:3–14 begins and ends with an allusion to a central goal of God's in the Old Testament: God has "chose[n] us [for himself] . . . to be holy and blameless before him" (Eph. 1:4) who are his "*own possession*" (Eph. 1:14 NASB). By beginning and ending with this central Old Testament theme of God having a holy people as his special possession, Paul was thus affirming that God has now realized this goal through the gospel of Jesus Christ. Surprisingly, this holy people includes both Jews and non-Jewish Gentiles together in one body since both groups receive the same graces, gifts, and benefits of Christ's sacrifice and the promised Holy Spirit. So, Ephesians 1:1–14 presents us with a summary of God's plan for humanity, which fulfills God's heart intention as found in the Old Testament.

ONE

Paul's Conduit Piping

Ephesians 1:1–2 *Paul, an apostle of Christ Jesus by the will of God, To the saints who are in Ephesus and are faithful in Christ Jesus: ²Grace to you and peace from God our Father and the Lord Jesus Christ.*

Understanding the Word. We can think of the apostle Paul as someone laying down electrical conduit piping, connecting people to God. Of course, God had started the connection and energized and electrified the connection through Jesus. But Paul's work was to lay down more and more line, to bring more and more people into contact with God and to help them stay connected and properly grounded. Even though some people thought Paul was running his own business, Paul understood himself to have been "sent out" directly by the Boss—that is what the word "apostle" means. An apostle is an official representative of someone superior; Paul understood his superior to be the Master Electrician, Christ Jesus. Now, the interesting thing about Paul was that he was initially an unwilling worker. He rabidly (think, "big dog foaming at the mouth") persecuted the church (see Acts 8:1–3), but then was converted and accepted his important role as an apostle, representing Jesus to others. This was his official capacity. Paul was so convinced of this fact that he could say, "Be imitators of me, as I am of Christ" (1 Cor. 11:1).

For Paul to be an apostle and represent Jesus, connecting people to God, took some guts. Okay, lots of guts. But Paul understood that he was acting according to God's will. God stood behind him. What Paul meant by this is that God had dramatically called him to a special task, to preach the gospel to all the nations. We can read about his calling and God's purpose for him in Acts 9:15–16. God had prepared, authorized, sent, and packaged Paul to preach the good news of Jesus Christ.

Now, how exactly did Paul help people stay connected to God in Jesus? Well, he did so through evangelizing and teaching them. But afterward, he had to leave to lay down more conduit elsewhere. So, he would send coworkers back to check up on his work; he would also return himself, as he was able (between jobs). But a very important way that he would help to keep people connected was through writing letters. Letters can convey the heart of a person, and have the benefit of being read again and read again and read again, to more and more people.

So, Paul was a letter writer. Paul's letters began in the standard way, by indicating sender(s) and recipient(s). Here in 1:1 we see that Paul was sending the letter alone, with no one else, which was not always the case (compare Galatians 1:1–2 and 2 Corinthians 1:1). We may assume that he had a letter secretary to write for him; and he indicated that he was writing as a prisoner (see Ephesians 3:1, 13). He wrote to "the saints" (1:1), or "the holy ones."

What can be communicated by the simple greeting "Grace . . . and peace"? Most people may not realize that this greeting is multicultural: it involved a converted Greek greeting ("grace") along with a Jewish greeting ("peace"). Paul made clear that the grace and peace he offered was from the Boss (God the Father) and the Boss's Son (the Lord Jesus Christ). So, importantly, Paul began each of his letters by acknowledging both Greek and Jewish cultures and identifying who lies behind the grace and the peace. You will see these two terms several more times as you read through Ephesians.

1. How far did Paul go to represent Jesus to other people? How far do you go?

2. How did Paul help people get connected to God and stay connected to God?

3. How might your greetings be more inclusive of others to convey God's grace and peace?

T W O

The Blessings of Being Back in the Family

Ephesians 1:3–6 *Blessed be the God and Father of our Lord Jesus Christ, who has blessed us in Christ with every spiritual blessing in the heavenly places, ⁴just as he chose us in Christ before the foundation of the world to be holy and blameless before him in love. ⁵He destined us for adoption as his children through Jesus Christ, according to the good pleasure of his will, ⁶to the praise of his glorious grace that he freely bestowed on us in the Beloved.*

Understanding the Word. Paul leads us, like a worship leader, to praise God. We are asked to join Paul in attributing blessedness to God. It is worth pausing to think about how greatly God is blessed and to be blessed. God is the source of all blessings that flow through Jesus Christ. In many ways, the entire epistle of Ephesians elaborates on the multidimensional nature of the blessings that come from God, the Father of our Lord Jesus Christ, first mentioned here in 1:3. It is important for us to understand that the blessedness offered to us is relational—it is not material; too often, we selfishly (let's just admit it!) think in material terms. But we must pay attention to how Paul delineated God's blessings here, which are spiritual and in the heavenly realms. The blessings pertain to belonging, having a significant purpose, and being caught up in something worthwhile that is bigger than ourselves. The good news of Jesus delivers on these blessings. Here we will focus on the blessing of belonging.

We belong. We are family; we are God's children when we are adopted into God's family. There is nothing that we could add to make this happen; God has provided it all. God has made it happen, and God invites our embrace of the truth on the matter. I find that this reality—my adoption into God's loving presence and family—is the core of my struggle in this world. It is hard to accept it freely; I want to earn it, to confirm it, to legitimate and justify myself in it. However, God supplies all the legitimacy, all the sufficiency, all the grace for this complete reality even to occur.

In the ancient Greco-Roman world, there was no stigma attached with adoption whatsoever, which carried with it the full rights of parental access and inheritance. Even the emperors Augustus, Tiberius, and Nero, living in the first century, were gladly adopted—it allowed each to become the reigning new emperor! As Paul explained, believers in Christ will reign with Jesus, seated in the heavenly realms with him, experiencing the wealth of God's grace and kindness (see 2:6–7)! So, as important as adoption is, it matters more *whose* you are, *whose* family you belong to, and *who* else belongs with you. The good news is that God has placed Jesus at the head of the family—each of us stands accountable to him and each of us stands equal before him. Your family line, your ancestry, your history are all made relative to God's history and God's family. It was God's plan all along (even as God foresaw our falling from grace) gladly to adopt us all back into the family as his children.

But the fact that we *must* be adopted back into the family presupposes that we all first find ourselves estranged and outside the family of God. Indeed, we are outside, if left to our own vices (see 2:1–3; 4:17–19). But God is fully pleased, fully prepared, to adopt us back into the family, fully ready to extend grace to each of us, to make the transaction official and true—that is what the Holy Spirit signifies to us, that we belong (see 1:14). This restoration and reentry can only happen because of the beloved Son, Jesus. And so our role in all this is to receive the grace, to come home, to receive the blessings and give praise for the glorious grace that restores us back to God, back to our family responsibilities to be holy and blameless in love before God. God likes this, because he "wants all people to be saved" (1 Tim. 2:4 NIV).

1. How does your understanding of blessedness match with Paul's statements here?

2. What characteristics of God lead you to praise him? Why does Paul lead us to praise God?

3. What does it mean that God wants you and everyone else to be in his family? How is this possible?

THREE

Christ's Sacrifice Reveals God's Will

Ephesians 1:7–10 *In him we have redemption through his blood, the forgiveness of our trespasses, according to the riches of his grace* *⁸that he lavished on us. With all wisdom and insight* *⁹he has made known to us the mystery of his will, according to his good pleasure that he set forth in Christ,* *¹⁰as a plan for the fullness of time, to gather up all things in him, things in heaven and things on earth.*

Understanding the Word. We have "redemption" through Christ's blood. This term refers to a purchase or a ransom paid. We were held captive, and God bailed us out. We receive forgiveness for our missteps, for our transgressions, for our hurtful actions. God's buy-back plan, however, doesn't leave us where we were. We are set free. When someone is ransomed, he or she is released. We don't pay the large sum of money only to leave someone captive. This is how God does it too. In fact, God's transaction to redeem and forgive corresponds with the great wealth of his grace—his grace is bottomless and limitless.

So much of our walk with God depends on his grace. But the good news is that God is not stingy with it. Instead, as 1:8 indicates, he "lavished [it] on us." God is like the Father who receives back a rebellious son living on the streets; although that son would be content to remain well fed with a roof over his head, God lavishes upon us the full restoration of relationship so that we can know for certain that we are his sons and daughters (see 2 Corinthians 6:18).

But is grace experienced if it is not known? Jesus Christ is the linchpin to God's grace revealed; Christ is God's marvelous and mysterious instrument of revelation. In the middle of verse 8, the prepositional phrase "With all wisdom and insight" should be understood as modifying "lavished . . . us"; there should be no period before it. Grace becomes lavished to the extent that the person knows about it, and elsewhere in Scripture this is affirmed. Peter said, "Grace and peace *be multiplied* to you *in the knowledge of God and of Jesus our Lord*" (2 Peter 1:2 NKJV; emphasis added). The more we know about God and Jesus and what they have done for us, the more we understand God's grace. God doesn't want it to be a mystery; it's for our good that grace is revealed.

At the core of it, God has freed us from the darkness and revealed himself. That is the nature of God: to reveal, but yet not to force himself and his ways onto us. He respects our distance, but in the midst of a crisis, he presents himself to save us. When we watch children play with other children, we may sometimes need to let the playing get ugly to see how it resolves (it's not easy to do!). Why? Because important lessons are learned. But we watch intently, ready to come in to save. Just when and how God has chosen to save is marvelous for us to ponder—because God shows a new way to be in the world that does not involve hating and killing our enemies. Instead, the good pleasure of God's will is to save; he wants all people to be saved. Christ is the linchpin to this plan, the one fulfilling God's plan to reconcile all things to himself.

1. How does your understanding of God's grace match up with Paul's description here?

2. How do you understand God to be active in the world, yet respecting our free will?

3. How is Jesus the linchpin to God's saving work?

FOUR

Inheritance Rights and Privileges

Ephesians 1:11–12 *In Christ we have also obtained an inheritance, having been destined according to the purpose of him who accomplishes all things according to his counsel and will, ¹²so that we, who were the first to set our hope on Christ, might live for the praise of his glory.*

Understanding the Word. For those living in poverty, who have no land of their own, who are out of the mainstream of power and influence, whose family may have abandoned them altogether—Paul's opening statement in 1:11 would be unbelievable: "we have also obtained an inheritance." This is too good to be true! I suspect that most of us who are reading this OneBook study cannot fully understand the magnitude of the statement. But in Paul's day, a good number of people—the majority of those living in the Mediterranean world—had no such hope. They were renters, squatters, or slaves, with no hope of making any real gains in the world, let alone having any inheritance that meant anything. And yet, in support of this claim that we have obtained an inheritance, Paul piled up descriptors such as "destined," "purpose," "accomplishes all things," "counsel," and "will." What he was trying to communicate is that *our inheritance is as certain as it gets.*

But what kind of inheritance are we talking about? We need to remember the context and where he will further describe our future (see esp. 2:4–7). Paul began and ended 1:3–14 with references to God's plan to have a "holy" people as his "own possession" (NET). The Old Testament texts that Paul had in mind are from Exodus and Deuteronomy, where God was giving the Law as a covenant agreement with Abraham's descendants for living in the new land. Moses was addressing Israel just as the Jewish nation was ready to take possession of this inheritance that God had granted. Under the Mosaic covenant, the inheritance was the land of Israel; however, as God sent prophets to help the people of Israel understand more and more his purposes, it becomes more and more clear that the inheritance is the whole earth, and not simply one strip of land. Moreover, the land was simply a covenant benefit that now has been expanded.

Was God more concerned about the land inheritance or the people inheriting the land? All along God has been more interested in having a people uniquely his own. The gift of the land was always subordinate to God's larger plan of having a holy people who would be numerous and would bless the nations. In Christ, there is a return to God's original purposes to inhabit the whole earth and bless the nations. Thus, Jesus said, "Blessed are the gentle, for they shall inherit the earth" (Matt. 5:5 NASB). Just when and how this inheritance will happen is in God's hands, but it will extend for ages and ages (see Ephesians 2:6–7); our responsibility here and now is to be faithful in carrying out God's purposes.

The purpose of God's gift of inheriting is expressed in 1:12. Paul used a very marked Greek construction to express this: "in order that we, who were the first to put our hope in Christ, might be for the praise of his glory" (NIV). Here, I think, Paul affirmed a fundamental aspect of human existence: we were made for relationship with God that involves bringing glory to God. Humans are manifestations of God's image, and to the extent that we reflect that image, we reflect the glory of God's image. When God adopts us back into his family and establishes our certain inheritance, we respond by praising him. This is our privilege as fully restored sons and daughters.

1. What inheritance do you look forward to?

2. How are you able to trust the certainty of God's will and purposes?

3. What are ways that you live for the praise of God's glory?

FIVE

Marked for Life

Ephesians 1:13–14 *In him you also, when you had heard the word of truth, the gospel of your salvation, and had believed in him, were marked with the seal of the promised Holy Spirit; ¹⁴this is the pledge of our inheritance toward redemption as God's own people, to the praise of his glory.*

Understanding the Word. Paul began verse 13 with another "in him," referring to Jesus Christ. Throughout 1:3–14 Paul used this and equivalent expressions eleven times. Indeed, Christ is the key that unlocks God's will and divulges God's plan. Paul here singled out the audience as "you also." It's as if he added them here explicitly into the conversation that they had been hearing. He particularly had in mind non-Jews, or Gentiles, whom he affirmed as also included among God's "own people," in Greek literally, God's "acquired possession." This fact—that non-Jews are now included in God's plans explicitly—was good news.

So important was this news that Paul described the exact steps involved in the process of the Gentiles' conversion to Christ: first *hearing*, then *believing*, then *being marked* with the seal of the promised Holy Spirit. What they *heard* was "the word of truth" further described as "the gospel of . . . salvation." The word "gospel" referred to the announcement of political good news such as when there was a military victory or when a new king was inaugurated. Well,

Jesus won the victory over sin, oppression, and death in the world and brought salvation; and Jesus was indeed heralded as King of kings and Lord of lords. That Paul referred to this good news as "the word of truth" reminds us that the gospel is objectively true, not just subjectively true for some people in some places and times. The gospel is true for all people; it brings God's salvation to everyone—there is no restriction to race, ethnicity, gender, social status, or any other label by which we could subdivide and categorize people. The gospel is enjoyed by non-Jews also, the Gentiles and the nations. God is not a respecter of persons, but loves and seeks after all people. Jesus came to seek and save what was lost (see Luke 19:10).

The next step in the process is *believing*. The verb for "believing" has more to do with trusting and being convinced of something on a good basis than with blind faith. So, believing is not simply intellectual assent, but active trusting, where one is all in and fully committed. Of course, we believers will grow more and more into this complete trust as we experience God as faithful. God shows himself again and again as trustworthy

Finally, the last step is *being marked* with the Holy Spirit. This verb designates the official marking of documents with signet rings for various legal purposes: wills, letters, receipts, and so forth. By analogy, believers get officially marked, which is a pledge or guarantee of their future inheritance. Paul here described the coming of the Holy Spirit as "sealing" believers. Some people will misunderstand this sealing to mean that believers are locked in and cannot turn away from God; they miss the metaphor. We are legitimate and official, bearing God's mark. Scripture is clear that people who have shared in the Holy Spirit can tragically walk away from the Lord (see Hebrews 6:4–6). In Ephesians Paul used the verb "sealed" to stress the official, royal, divine marking of the believers (esp. Gentiles) to signify their authenticity. There is no doubt whose we are and to whom we belong. Moreover, the Holy Spirit empowers believers to truly live "to the praise of [God's] glory."

1. How is the gospel good news for all people?

2. Why would Paul stress the official legitimacy of believers, and especially Gentile believers?

3. What in life most leaves its mark on you? In what way does God want to leave his mark on you?

WEEK ONE

GATHERING DISCUSSION OUTLINE

A. Open session in prayer.

B. View video for this week's readings.

C. What general impressions and thoughts do you have after considering the video, readings, and the daily writings on these Scriptures?

D. Discuss questions based on the daily readings.

1. **KEY OBSERVATION**: God has gone to extremes to reach out to people. Jesus called Paul, a persecutor of God's people, to become an apostle. He equipped him and sent him out. Then Paul represented Jesus Christ to others. As he wrote letters, he acknowledged different cultural greetings, but in greeting Jew and Gentile, he pointed them to God the Father and the Lord Jesus Christ.

   DISCUSSION QUESTION: How did Paul help people get connected to God and stay connected to God?

2. **KEY OBSERVATION**: God's blessings flow out of Jesus Christ. They are particularly spiritual in nature and in the heavenly realms. God has strategically placed Jesus in the heavenly realms for our benefit. One particular blessing is God's realization of having a people that are holy and blameless in love. Such a people have been adopted back into God's family as full sons and daughters of God, with all the rights, privileges, and responsibilities appertaining thereto.

   DISCUSSION QUESTION: What does it mean that God wants you and everyone else to be in his family? How is this possible?

3. **KEY OBSERVATION**: God's grace saves us, but in a vulnerable way. It was costly, but God was well pleased to send Christ into the world to die for us and pay the ransom. In this costly act, God's will is revealed. Christ is the key to how God saves. We need to keep looking at how God has revealed his will, because as we continue learning, we come more and more to understand God's lavishing of grace upon us.

   DISCUSSION QUESTION: How does your understanding of God's grace match up with Paul's description here?

4. **KEY OBSERVATION**: We have obtained an inheritance that we can be assured of. Although it is kept for us in the future, its scope is large: the entire world. God has longed to have a people that are his people. Jesus came as the Messiah to form a people that would belong to God. God's purpose all along is that his people would praise his glory.

   DISCUSSION QUESTION: What inheritance do you look forward to?

5. **KEY OBSERVATION**: The good news is for all people. Gentiles are included with the Jewish nation in receiving the gospel, which announces both Jesus' victory over sin, oppression, and death and the inauguration of God's kingdom. Believers in Jesus are marked with the promised Holy Spirit when they hear and believe the Word of truth. The Spirit designates that believers are official and legitimate. The Spirit guarantees that they belong to God as his "acquired possession" that leads to living for the praise of God's glory.

   DISCUSSION QUESTION: What in life most leaves its mark on you? In what way does God want to leave his mark on you?

E. What facts and information presented in the commentary portion of the lesson help you understand the weekly Scripture?

F. Close session with prayer.

Ephesians 1:15–23

Paul's Thanksgiving and Prayer for Revelation

INTRODUCTION

One of the great joys that believers have is to lift up one another before the Lord in prayer. We stand in the great tradition of God's people who have interceded for one another and also for the blessings of those not yet believers. Such prayer is a priestly act inasmuch as we stand in the gap between God and others. In this regard, we follow in Jesus' footsteps, who also stood between God and others, praying and acting for their good. He is our great High Priest; we are little priests, who come to God in prayer, interceding for ourselves, those closest to us, and those far away.

While prayer has wonderful benefits for the one praying, perhaps the most important benefit is the expanded vision of life for others that prayer entails. First, when we pray, we begin to gain a vision of the truly Other—God himself. We enjoy relationship with God in Christ through the Holy Spirit as we offer ourselves in prayer. Second, in praying, we look to the good of other believers and of people not yet in the faith. As we grow in knowledge of God and God's will as revealed in Scripture, God will help shape our praying according to his purposes, which includes saving all people; our praying becomes a participation with God in his saving activities (see esp. 1 Timothy 2:1–4).

In Ephesians 1:15–23, we are privy to seeing Paul pray for the believers in and around Ephesus. He prayed for them to see the wonderful, glorious future that God had in store for them; he prayed for them to see the power God has revealed in resurrecting Jesus and placing him in a position of power "far above all rule and authority and power and dominion, and above every name that is named, not only in this age but also in the age to come" (Eph. 1:21). In the devotion that follows, we will consider why Paul prayed the way he did.

ONE

No Stopping Giving Thanks

Ephesians 1:15–16 *I have heard of your faith in the Lord Jesus and your love toward all the saints, and for this reason* [16]*I do not cease to give thanks for you as I remember you in my prayers.*

Understanding the Word. Christians live in community with one another. We hear things. We pay attention to things. What we pay attention to and what we care to hear will be clearly evident by our response to what we pay attention to and hear. In these two verses, we are privileged to see what Paul cared about and how he responded to it. Paul was paying attention to people's faith in the Lord Jesus Christ and their love for all the saints, that is, believers both Jewish and Gentile. Believing in Jesus and loving others: that effectively sums up the core of the Christian life. The latter flows out of the former. Love results from trusting in Jesus, since we learn our needs for love and forgiveness and then reflect back that love for others. Paul in Ephesians will have much to say about love in the chapters that follow.

In response to hearing of the Ephesians' faith and love, Paul continually prayed for them. In this way, Paul remained in relationship with people, even when he was not physically present with them. You see, Paul was constantly on the move, traveling from place to place, yet he understood how to stay well-connected and to foster togetherness even at a distance. He remembered. Paul is here showing us a fundamental dimension of how to live life together as believers in Christ. Our life together contains many important elements: worship, sharing meals, helping one another in need, encouragement, study, recreation, and outreach. However, a privilege that we enjoy with one another is to share a life of prayer one for another as we remember one another. This practice of remembering maintains and even fosters relationships. Believers support each other in many ways, but most importantly through prayer. It is not accidental that most of Paul's letters began with a description of Paul's praying for believers.

What is prayer? It is conversing with God. It is a two-way conversation—talking but also listening. As with any good friend, there is mutual exchange of giving and receiving. Prayer is thus important for us because it maintains our relationship with God. However, when we pray for others, we stand in the middle between God and others and take on the role of a mediator, as certainly Jesus Christ was. Jesus himself modeled this life of prayer. Before dying, he offered up a prayer to God the Father for himself, for the disciples, and for future believers (see John 17). This is often called Jesus' High Priestly Prayer. There is some real sense that believers become like priests as we pray for one another: we stand in the gap for one another. I like to think of prayer as a triangulation—we connect others to God. When believers pray, they are especially like Christ and his priestly role of representing others before God, bringing others into God's presence.

1. What do you pay attention to and listen to? What actions do you take in response?

2. How are ways that we can hear or learn of someone's faith? What is your response to their faith?

3. If giving thanks for people results from remembering them while praying, how important is remembering?

TWO

Wisdom and Revelation

Ephesians 1:17 *I pray that the God of our Lord Jesus Christ, the Father of glory, may give you a spirit of wisdom and revelation as you come to know him,*

Understanding the Word. Here in 1:17 we see the beginning of what Paul was praying for, that is, the content of his prayer. At the core is that we would be given by God a "spirit of wisdom and revelation." Another way to translate "spirit" would be "disposition"; what Paul was praying for was that believers would have an inner disposition and focus on wisdom and the revelation of who God is. Wisdom refers to knowledge and understanding for proper living. Wisdom and good living go hand in hand. The revelation concerns God; knowing God is revelatory—we learn about the nature of life and the universe. We learn how things work from the insider's perspective. God is the ultimate Insider, and he wants us to be on the inside of the action, understanding as much as needed to be effective as his agents on a mission.

But even before the prayer's content, Paul affirmed who the Giver is: "The God of our Lord Jesus Christ" who is "the Father of glory." Paul will continue to name-drop "God" and "Jesus" throughout Ephesians. It is really quite remarkable, and we need to pay attention to this and understand. So, why did Paul keep mentioning God and Jesus and describing who they are? We might suppose that Paul thought his readers had short memories or limited attention spans. Well, that is not quite right. Instead, we need to understand that these early believers had deep-seated memories of many other gods and goddesses: Greek ones, Roman ones, and local ones. You may have heard of them; recently in American culture there has been a resurgence of interest through fantasy books and movies. This might seem rather strange to us, but not when we realize how commonly images of gods and goddesses dominated the early church's lives.

Back then, images of these gods and goddesses were seen across various media, such as statuary in temples or shrines, images on coins or household utensils, mosaics and paintings on walls and floors, and reliefs on walls, gateway arches, and so forth. Moreover, the gods were celebrated at festivals, sacrifices, parades, dramatic competitions, and athletic contests. Basically, these gods and goddesses permeated the world of the first believers. Thus, these pagan images were constantly calling for people's attention. People then had a "gods folder" in their mind's eye. So, this explains why Paul constantly named and identified God and Jesus—he was attempting to (re)populate each member's gods folder with a singular God folder. However, this is also beneficial for us, since we have our own folders for God with true, partially true, or sometimes simply wrong knowledge of God; or we may have no God folder and so we each need to have our individual God folders properly populated and informed.

For now, let's focus on what Paul has drawn our attention to in 1:17. God is "the Father of glory," which means that he is the originator of all honor and fame. He is the reference point for all that is worthy of honor, fame, and glory. Also, he gives us Jesus, who is "the Christ." This designation indicated that Jesus was the long-awaited and hoped-for Jewish King. The Jewish people had been expecting God to send a King who would deliver them from their enemies. Jesus is also identified as "Lord," which indicates his divine status as well as his authority.

1. How would you distinguish wisdom and revelation? Why are these important?

2. Do you have a God folder? What is in your God folder?

3. How does someone come to know God? What are the ways?

THREE

God's Great Power

Ephesians 1:18–19 *so that, with the eyes of your heart enlightened, you may know what is the hope to which he has called you, what are the riches of his glorious inheritance among the saints,* [19]*and what is the immeasurable greatness of his power for us who believe, according to the working of his great power.*

Understanding the Word. Knowledge begets more knowledge. The more you know, the more you can know—there is a cumulative effect. As we get to know God better and better, we are able to understand more and more. In the first part of 1:18, Paul explained the mechanism for how this takes place. It is deeply seated within us. It is in the eyes of our hearts. Paul used a metaphor, since anatomically we know that our eyes are in our heads and not our hearts. But what Paul described here is an inner vision that comes from within us, from the very center of our lives. We have been enlightened, and our vision at the deepest core of our being is able to see more and more. This deep enlightenment comes from the Holy Spirit and helps us to know God more and more. It is not that we receive more and more of God—when we come to faith, we receive God, Jesus, and the Holy Spirit. It's just that in our thinking and understanding, there is a need to learn more and more and to grow in our relationship with God. In this regard, coming to know God is like getting to know a person—there is a lot to know, and it takes time!

17

In 1:18–19 we see the goal of Paul's prayer; the "so that" indicates this purpose. It may be helpful for you to know that when Paul prayed for believers at the beginning of his letters, the content of these prayers provided an overview of important themes that he would touch upon later in the letter. This is rather interesting, too, because we see that Paul participated in the answer to his prayers! He didn't just pray; he did something about his praying! This is a lesson for us; prayer prepares us for action. In other words, if we pray for something to occur, we are likely being prepared to do something about it. We see this, for example, when Jesus asked the disciples to pray to God to send out workers for the harvest (that is, to pray for people to reach out to other people). Then, in the next verses, Jesus sent them out to spread the good news (see Matthew 9:37–10:7).

Here we need to notice the three "whats" that form a list: (1) what is the hope to which he has called you, (2) what are the riches of his glorious inheritance among the saints, and (3) what is the immeasurable greatness of his power for us who believe. God enables us to understand a lot—by giving us an enlightened heart, it is possible for us to know God's hope for us, God's glorious inheritance, and God's great power for us. The first two in the list are future-time oriented. That is, they relate to the future. However, "hope" is an attitude that we maintain about the future. Hope encourages us in the present with a vision of the future. Paul in Ephesians will describe aspects of this hope and inheritance in 2:4–7; 4:13–17; and 5:5. However, Paul will especially focus on the "greatness of [God's] power for us who believe." We will see this in the next verses. For now we need to understand that this empowerment is what enables believers to live differently in the world and to fulfill God's purposes. Also, it was first displayed in Christ's life.

1. How have the eyes of your heart been enlightened? What are you seeing deeply?

2. What are you praying for, and how might you be in the process of being prepared to participate in answering the prayer?

3. Which of the three "whats" is most pressing and important to you now?

FOUR

Raised above All Rule and Authority

Ephesians 1:20–21 *God put this power to work in Christ when he raised him from the dead and seated him at his right hand in the heavenly places, ²¹far above all rule and authority and power and dominion, and above every name that is named, not only in this age but also in the age to come.*

Understanding the Word. Of the three "whats" in Paul's prayer (vv. 18–19), the last one receives the greatest explanation. Paul spent considerable time telling us about God's power. At the end of 1:19, he used the expression "according to the working of his great power." In the original Greek language, Paul used three different words for "power." He was stressing the greatness of God's power displayed.

First, God's power was focused in Jesus Christ. In Jesus' earthly life, the power assisted Jesus as he lived—he had discernment, he preached the gospel in the midst of conflict, he performed healings and miracles, and he coura-geously faced death when he went to Jerusalem and confronted the injustices of the religious leaders of his day.

Second, God's power was manifested in a way never seen before by raising Jesus' dead body from the grave. This is called the *resurrection*. In the resurrec-tion, God testified that Jesus was the Messiah; he brought life back into Jesus' corpse and gave him a glorious new body. Although the Bible tells us of people being resuscitated from the dead (only to die again) or being seen no more (like Enoch, who was presumably "translated" somehow into God's presence), Jesus is the only one resurrected from the dead never to die again. This is good news for us, because it means that God has overcome death. As I like to say, "Death is not the end of us!"

Third, God's power was displayed in seating Jesus at his right hand. Not only was Jesus raised from the dead, but he ascended to heaven to occupy the highest position of power. This is called the *ascension*. The ascension refers to Jesus, after his resurrection, being taken up to heaven to be with the Father "at his right hand." This fulfilled Scripture. Paul here alluded to Psalm 110:1, which describes King David's "Lord" coming up to sit at God's right hand.

Psalm 110 is one of the most commonly cited or alluded to Old Testament passages in the entire New Testament—it is that important! (See, for example, Luke 22:69; Acts 7:55–56; Romans 8:34; Colossians 3:1; Hebrews 1:3; 8:1; 10:12; 12:2; 1 Peter 3:22.)

Fourth, God seated Jesus "in the heavenly places, far above all rule and authority." This is fighting language, so to speak, since people then believed the heavenly places to be occupied by the strongest gods and goddesses, and even the deceased emperors, including Augustus! Yes, emperors were thought to have come from the heavens and then to die and return there in spirit. It was part of their understanding of the world. Rulers came from heaven. However, Paul showed that God raised and elevated Jesus to the highest position of power, above all others. Not only that, but also Christ remains above "every name that is named, not only in this age but also in the age to come," that is, for all time, now and forevermore. What this means is that we as believers are well-connected to the Power Source and to the Ultimate Position of Power. God approves of Jesus, and we should follow after him. This power assists us to carry out God's purpose and mission in the world, which Paul will explain as the letter continues.

1. In what way was God's power most evident in Jesus?

2. Why is knowing about God's power in Jesus important for us?

3. What official position does Christ now occupy, and why is this significant?

FIVE

Right Rule

Ephesians 1:22–23 *And he has put all things under his feet and has made him the head over all things for the church, ²³which is his body, the fullness of him who fills all in all.*

Understanding the Word. In 1:22, Paul continued to explain what God had accomplished in raising Jesus from the dead and seating him at the right hand of power, far above all other rule and authority. Paul did so by alluding to

Psalm 8:6. This psalm explains God's purpose for humans to rule the earth. Here is the verse in context of Psalm 8:4–8.

> What are human beings that you are mindful of them,
>> mortals that you care for them?
> Yet you have made them a little lower than God,
>> and crowned them with glory and honor.
> You have given them dominion over the works of your hands;
>> you have put all things under their feet,
> all sheep and oxen,
>> and also the beasts of the field,
> the birds of the air, and the fish of the sea,
>> whatever passes along the paths of the seas.

What Paul recognized is that Jesus has fulfilled the human (pre)occupation of ruling the world. This takes us back to the book of Genesis and how God gave dominion to Adam and Eve over all the world. The problem is that we humans, in our attempts at living in the world and fulfilling this goal, rejected God in the process; instead of following God's ways and honoring God's position as God, we attempted to "make a name for ourselves" (Gen. 11:4) and create our own tower ascending into the heavens. This first city, with its tower, was called Babel (see Genesis 11). The human problem, you see, is a political problem; hence, it requires a political solution. God's solution is in providing Jesus as our Ruler, who shows us a different way of being in the world. Jesus fulfills the human calling, and then invites us to join with him in completing the task. For this reason, it is better to translate 1:23 this way: "which is his body, the fulfillment of the One who fulfills all things in every way."

But let's think a bit more about Paul's description of Jesus as having feet, head, and body. Such bodily language draws from a common political metaphor in the ancient world (see also 1 Corinthians 12:12–28). Significantly, the church is the body of Christ. It belongs to Christ organically. The church is part of Christ, and Christ the church. It is really quite impossible to separate them. We belong together; it is not unnatural. In fact, it is most natural for a head to have a body, and we are Christ's body. God has placed Christ in the supreme position of rule and power as the Head "over all things," and this has been done "for the church," that is, for the benefit of the church. This is amazing! Christ oversees all things as "the head," which also indicates the "source" of everything. In English usage, we also use "head" with such a meaning: the head of a river is the source of the river. Also, it is important to understand that at this time, the Roman emperor Nero was considered the soul or head of the Roman people, the body, as the source of all sorts of benefits for them. Paul was once again countering the prevailing ideas of his age that were detrimental to believers. One problem with humans is having bad political rulers that lead them in the wrong directions. Not so with Christ.

1. What was God's original creative design for humanity?

2. How does Jesus fulfill God's design for humanity? How does the church do so?

3. What temptations face humanity?

WEEK TWO

GATHERING DISCUSSION OUTLINE

A. Open session in prayer.

B. View video for this week's readings.

C. What general impressions and thoughts do you have after considering the video, readings, and the daily writings on these Scriptures?

D. Discuss questions based on the daily readings.

    1. **KEY OBSERVATION**: Christians live in community with one another. A privilege that we enjoy with one another is to share a life of prayer for one another as we remember each other. This practice of remembering maintains and even fosters relationships. Believers support each other in many ways, but most importantly through prayer.

    DISCUSSION QUESTION: If giving thanks for people results from remembering them while praying, how important is remembering?

    2. **KEY OBSERVATION**: We each have conceived of the world in various ways and may or may not have a God folder. Regardless, when we come to faith in God in Jesus Christ, we are given a new God folder and learn more and more about God. God wants to share true information to include in the folder and enables believers to grow in their understanding of God.

    DISCUSSION QUESTION: Do you have a God folder? What is in your God folder?

3. **KEY OBSERVATION**: Knowledge begets more knowledge. The more you know, the more you can know. God has enlightened the hearts of believers to know more and more. Paul prayed for the believers in Ephesus to know about God's hope and inheritance for them, but especially God's power for them. In response to his own prayer, Paul writes the letter to explain more about the nature of God's hope and inheritance.

   DISCUSSION QUESTION: What are you praying for and how might you be being prepared to participate in answering the prayer?

4. **KEY OBSERVATION**: God's power is most evidently displayed in that God has raised Jesus from the dead and seated him "in the heavenly places, far above all rule and authority." Such a statement countered the common view in the Roman world of the gods, goddesses, and emperors being within and controlling such space and position. Rather, Christ rules above them all now and forevermore. Thus, believers are well-connected to God's Power and approved Ruler, Jesus.

   DISCUSSION QUESTION: What official position does Christ now occupy and why is this significant?

5. **KEY OBSERVATION**: God's placement of all things under the feet of Jesus fulfills God's plan for humanity. In as much as people join Jesus' body, they fulfill God's plan, too. Alternatively, people are often mislead by political leaders and thus fail to fulfill God's designs. Jesus is our model for living in the world.

   DISCUSSION QUESTION: How does Jesus fulfill God's design for humanity? How does the church do so?

E. What facts and information presented in the commentary portion of the lesson help you understand the weekly Scripture?

F. Close session with prayer.

Ephesians 2:1–10

Our Sinful Plight Meets God's Gift of Salvation

INTRODUCTION

Following the wonderful vision of Christ fulfilling humanity's purpose, we find a sobering depiction of human sin leading to death. Sin and death are bed partners; where you find one, the other is nearby. There are two kinds of death: (1) a physical ceasing and (2) a relational alienation, which we often refer to as a *spiritual death*. Both result from a problem that humans have that we label as "sin."

As Paul explained to the Ephesians here, there are several layers to the sin problem: an era spreading over the world, poor human rulers, a spirit opposed to God, people who are disobedient, sinful passions, fleshly wills, and anger management issues. However, the good news is that God meets us at our worst with his very best—love, mercy, and grace that saves us in giving us Jesus the Messiah. By grace we are saved, and this does not originate from ourselves. God meets us in order to save us and join us to himself. In fact, believers are made alive with Christ, raised with Christ, and seated with Christ in the heavenly realms (upon death). And God's provision to overcome death is only the beginning: his kindness will be expressed to us in the ages yet to come. But in the meantime, we remain here as a monument to God. We stay and follow in the footsteps of Jesus, walking in good deeds as we participate in God's plan of salvation.

ONE

Dead in Our Tracks

Ephesians 2:1–2 *You were dead through the trespasses and sins ²in which you once lived, following the course of this world, following the ruler of the power of the air, the spirit that is now at work among those who are disobedient.*

Understanding the Word. Paul now squarely addresses two uncomfortable topics: sin and death. However, they have already been assumed in the previous statements. In 1:5, he explained that God planned to adopt us, which presupposes that we at some point were not in his family but outside the family. That reflects sin; sin is the absence of good. It causes us to be separated from ourselves and others. Whether we know we sin or not, there is still a lacking of good in us that plagues us. In Romans 5:13–14, Paul explained that we know sin is present in the world because people die. Death and sin go together. Sometimes this is immediately the case, as in a murder or bombing. Some people will revel in sin and death; this defiant response is seen in what they wear and how they dress. But most people hide in their sin and try to avoid thinking about death. Which response is better? In God's eyes, each one has inherent value and can be adopted into the family.

Death has also already been mentioned in Ephesians. In 1:7, Paul explained that God's adoption plan comes at the cost of Christ's blood; it comes "through his blood." Nothing else is said there. We are worth the cost; but the death of Christ is the buyback, and we are worth every drop of it in God's eyes. But Jesus Christ is so much more than the buyback; he is also Lord and Head of the body and Savior. These are political titles, and our salvation includes being delivered from higher structures of reality that include the world, rulers, and spirits.

In 2:2, Paul begins to name things that provide the environment of our deadly, sinful life, things that, he said, the believers at Ephesus and its surrounding areas once followed, whether knowingly or unknowingly. He was speaking in terms they would understand; we will need to do some translation to bring some of the ideas into our own time period. The first thing listed is "following the course [or age] of this world." This is fairly straightforward; people live in societies, and the sinful patterns of living are reflected back at us:

we are expected to conform. It is often very subtle, especially the underlying ideology. Advertisements reflect this well, showing us images and telling us stories in order to persuade us to buy their products. They do so by appealing often to our worst self-oriented desires: power, glamour, sex, greed, and so on. But sometimes the appeal is to basic needs: love, respect, safety, and comfort. It is a mixed bag, but cultural patterns shape us for good and too often for bad.

The second, third, and fourth structures that Paul identified involve the political and spiritual realms. In the ancient world, these were inextricably linked. The Ephesians had followed "the ruler" which is related to "the power of the air, the spirit . . ." Interpreters will lump these two together under "Satan," who is the spirit that opposes God. But Paul did not name Satan here, and these are two different entities. So who are they? From my extensive research, I have discovered that "the ruler" is the emperor (at the time, Nero) and "the power of the air" signified Jupiter/Zeus, the topmost divinity in the ancient Greco-Roman world, who was thought to legitimate all human rule and controlled the air (lightning, rain, hail). Kings are established by Zeus. Both entities are unnamed, but the believers in Ephesians would have understood the references. But Paul effectively placed them off-limits; despite the widespread presence of both the emperor and Zeus, these were bad influences! They caused people to live disobediently.

1. How evident is sin and death in your life? Is this comfortable to discuss?

2. What are positive and negative appeals commonly seen in advertisements? Do these threaten our living for God?

3. How do political leaders influence people negatively? How is Christ the better example?

TWO

Passion and Anger Issues

Ephesians 2:3 *All of us once lived among them in the passions of our flesh, following the desires of flesh and senses, and we were by nature children of wrath, like everyone else.*

Understanding the Word. In 2:3, Paul switched to include himself in the mix. He was a Jew, and the Jews neither lived under the auspices of Zeus, nor followed the emperor. Yet, Jews were still under the influence of sin and trespassed against God's law, and so experienced death. Notice that Paul indicated that "all of us [including Jews] once lived among them." All people, whether Jew or Gentile, were in the same boat. They all rebelled against God at some level and experienced death. For the Jews, however, God had a different political plan. They had God as their Divinity, unlike the other nations, who were under the influence of other "gods" (see Deuteronomy 32:8–9); it was a pagan world out there, but not for the Jews. The Jewish confession was to live under the one God. Their confession was "Hear, O Israel: The LORD our God, the LORD *is* one!" (Deut. 6:4 NKJV). But despite this great divine heritage, despite being in covenant relationship with God and having the Law, the Jews also struggled with sin internally. In fact, God had provided a sacrificial system to deal with sin until he would establish a new relationship, a new covenant, which Jesus Christ brought, a new covenant that is better than the old covenant (see the book of Hebrews).

However, before this new covenant was put into place, the Law was given as a centerpiece of the old covenant, and the Jewish people were obligated to follow it. However, Paul explained that the Law only increased sin (see Romans 5:20). How? Well, the Law identified sin, gave it a name. And people transgressed it, broke it. In this regard, the Law was not unlike forbidding children to sneak cookies from the cookie jar. The Law gets broken and reveals the deeper problems. Sin runs very deep—so deep, in fact, that no external law or set of enforced behavioral modifications can treat it.

So here, Paul named the locations: "the passions of our flesh" and "the desires of flesh and senses." These ideas need some unpacking. Passions are deeply seated longings that are intricately linked to our bodies (the flesh). Even though our bodies are good and made to be good, under the influence of sin our bodies' longings become rather overwhelming and influence us to act badly, or sin. We each have had our moments of failing, in which we have given way to satisfy our longings, whether for power, influence, control, sex, hunger, or greed. These desires become lodged inside our bodies and often find a way of expression. Likewise, Paul described "desires"—a better translation here would be "wills," because it shows the conflict between the flesh and our senses (literally, "reasonings"); we are internally conflicted between multiple desires and wills.

In the end, Paul described the common fate of the Jews with all people: "we were . . . children of wrath, like everyone else." No one is better than anyone else; we each find ourselves in the same boat. Any finger-pointing is pointless (remember, there are three fingers pointing back at you!). The expression "children of wrath" may be understood in two ways. First, the word "wrath" or "anger" may describe the children—they are angry with each other. So, another translation might be "angry children." There is some great truth to this. Alternatively, "wrath" may describe the outcome of their sinful behavior— God's wrath. This is true also. But whose children are we at this point? The good news is that our sinfulness and death are overcome by God's merciful, loving, and graceful response in Christ Jesus. Paul will describe how in the next few verses.

1. How are Jews and Gentiles different yet alike with regard to sin and death?

2. Where does sin reside in people? How does it manifest itself?

3. What does it mean that people are "children of wrath"?

THREE

Together with Christ

Ephesians 2:4–6 *But God, who is rich in mercy, out of the great love with which he loved us *⁵even when we were dead through our trespasses, made us alive together with Christ—by grace you have been saved—⁶and raised us up with him and seated us with him in the heavenly places in Christ Jesus, . . .*

Understanding the Word. We need good news. After naming our sins and their consequences in black and white, Paul turned to God. Where else can we turn? Where else is there hope in the world? Paul's description of God's activity is rich and lavish. He is not stingy. Like the father of the prodigal son (see Luke 15:11–32), God lavishes upon us a full and complete restoration: we are adopted back into the family with full rights, benefits, and privileges.

How exactly does God meet our sinful condition? He treats us with love that manifests in mercy. Love is behind it all. Love is valuing the other as worthwhile. We are valuable and worthwhile even as we are sinful. In fact, it may be said that we sin to prove our own self-worth. The problem with that is that our worth comes from God! Any attempt to prove our worth apart from God is pointless and false. We were created by God; we are not our own. We belong to God; God owns our lease on life. Fortunately, God is not a stingy landlord; he has mercy and forgives. God's love is the foundation of his mercy. Mercy is not giving someone the punishment that he or she rightly deserves. We deserve to die everlastingly, but God forgives and provides another plan. God meets our deadness with his mercy. He shows us a better way of living in the world.

Paul provided three verbs to show how God meets our deadness; in the underlying Greek, each verb begins with the same sound (a preposition) that means "with" and stresses our belonging to Christ—it is very impactful to hear. These three verbs form a list: (1) God *made* us alive with Christ, (2) God *raised* us up with him, and (3) God *seated* us with him in the heavenly realms. We should notice that our living matches Christ's being resurrected and ascending to God's right hand. What God did for Christ, he also does for us out of his loving mercy and grace. We as readers of Ephesians have been prepared for this, since Paul devoted so much time describing the power of God in raising and seating Christ in the heavenly realms (see 1:19–20). Moreover, in that earlier statement Paul had affirmed that the church is the body of Christ (see 1:22–23); as such, it is not surprising, then, that Christ's body belongs with Christ, seated with him in the heavenly realms. We should remember that this is a place of ruling power far above all other rule and authority (see 1:21). So, 2:5–6 explain in more detail the close, intimate relationship that believers have as Christ's body.

But when does this take place? We should notice that Paul used past tense verbs to describe what God does for believers: *made* alive, *raised* up, and *seated*. Some interpreters see these verbs as timeless in the sense that they describe what is generally true metaphorically; believers are not really raised into the heavenly realms. However, it is best to understand that these have occurred for some and will continue to happen as believers die in the Lord. In other words, as we die, we go to be present with Jesus where he is; this is what Paul understood (see 2 Corinthians 5:8; Philippians 1:23). So, being made alive, being raised up, and being seated with Christ is what has happened to believers and what will happen to them as they die in the Lord. This is how God overcomes our deadly sin.

1. How and why has God shown sinful humans his mercy?

2. How easy—or not—is it to show mercy to ourselves or to others?

3. What specifically has God done to keep believers with Christ?

FOUR

Saved by Grace

Ephesians 2:7–9 *so that in the ages to come he might show the immeasurable riches of his grace in kindness toward us in Christ Jesus. ⁸For by grace you have been saved through faith, and this is not your own doing; it is the gift of God—⁹not the result of works, so that no one may boast.*

Understanding the Word. It is unfortunate to separate 2:7 from 2:4–6 because 2:7 is the purpose or goal for these earlier verses. We need to understand the underlying logic. In Ephesians, Paul often expressed ideas using a means-to-an-end logic, or what is called "purpose statements." Such statements are very important to observe because we learn a lot about what God has in mind, his intentions. What is God really after, anyway? What does he want to do with us and for us? Well, 2:7 is quite an important verse because it describes God's long-term plan for humanity. Sometimes people and couples will describe a one-, two-, or ten-year plan. They may even have a retirement plan. Verse 7 is God's eternal plan for us, and what a plan it is! God wants to show us "the immeasurable riches of his grace in kindness toward us in Christ Jesus." That is fantastic! Paul didn't describe what form exactly this will take, but we can trust that it will be good. In fact, this plan reflects God's kindness to us. This is amazing, because we are so undeserving! But this is how good God is.

At this point it is important to recognize that God does not deliver us from dying now; we will still suffer in this life (and quite a bit). We share in the life, death, and resurrection of Jesus completely. We are saved *through* death, not *from* it. This is important to ponder; we might ask why. It is difficult to answer this, but I am confident that we can trust in God's reasons. Let me suggest here that God knows what he is doing; he is working things for the best possible ends. He is working salvation for maximum outcome while still preserving our integrity to respond freely to him. He does not force himself on us; we can reject him. However, that would be foolish, especially in view of the wonderful forever plan that God has in store for us.

A repeated word in 2:5, 7, and 8 is the word "grace." We have already seen the word in 1:2 (the letter's greeting) and 1:6–8, where God's grace is lavished on us through his beloved Son, Jesus. Grace is unmerited favor; God's grace is the basis of our salvation. Paul stressed this point by repeating the statement "by grace you have been saved" in 2:5 and 2:8. Can grace be resisted? Absolutely. So, God's show of favor needs to be responded to by faith, by trust, by believing. That is the meaning of "through faith." Indeed, God helps us believe, but it still our believing and trusting that responds to God's grace. Really, believing in God is not foreign to us; many people believe in God at some level, or want to believe. What they need is clarity about who God is: how he loves them, has mercy for them, and forgives them in Christ. This is the gospel message of truth that the Ephesian believers heard and believed (see 1:13). This gospel message saves.

What is the source of our salvation? Paul clarified that it "is not your own doing." That is an important clarification. Nor is it "the result of works, so that no one may boast." As much as we might try to save ourselves, we cannot. Not even having God's law is enough (see Romans 2:17, 23–25). It is like trying to patch a sinking boat with a gaping hole from the inside—we just can't do it. Help must come from the outside. That's where God's gift comes in. Salvation "is the gift of God." The word used here for "gift" refers to sacrificial gifts. In Leviticus, such gifts were always human given, but not here! God's gift is Christ's sacrifice of giving and offering himself (see Ephesians 1:6; 5:2, 25).

1. What is God's long-term plan? Why did Paul describe it the way he did?

2. What is God's grace? How have you experienced grace?

3. How important is it that Paul explained in detail the source of our salvation? Why?

FIVE

Our Foundation in Christ

Ephesians 2:10 *For we are what he has made us, created in Christ Jesus for [upon] good works, which God prepared beforehand to be our way of life [in order that we would live in them].*

Understanding the Word. Within Ephesians, 2:8–10 provide a sketch for the rest of the letter. These verses are the thesis statement, so to speak. We learned in the previous day's devotion that grace is the basis of our salvation and is God's gift of Christ as our sacrifice. This was done so that no one could boast. For Paul to mention boasting might seem quite strange, but he was addressing the religious bigotry and favoritism that existed in Jesus' day, a form of which Jesus also addressed. God's historic people, as caretakers of the Law and the covenant, had come to believe that they were extra special; many of their leaders and writers spoke quite disparagingly of "others," that is, the pagan Gentiles. Paul immediately redressed this issue in 2:11–22, where he described how Christ overcame the animosity between Jew and Gentile. It is worth mentioning this now because it helps provide a framework to properly understand 2:10. Paul here addressed bigotry as expressed from the other vantage point, that of the Gentile world.

Let's start by looking at what the NRSV translates as "we are what he has made us." The underlying Greek language here is much simpler and to the point: "We are his [God's] workmanship/creation." Paul was making a political statement, since at the time when Paul wrote Ephesians, Rome as the capital of the world was described as the great(est) "work" or "creation" (in Latin, "opus") of their founders, especially the emperor Augustus. Rome boasted of its influence over the world. It had the gods' blessings. It was divinely favored. But Paul set forth God's alternative: Christ's body, the church. A political problem has a political solution.

Paul continued by affirming that the church was "created in Christ Jesus for [upon] good works." The verb "created" is too imprecise for this context. This verb and its related words were very commonly used for the founding of political institutions: people groups, colonies, cities, cults, and local groups. Lots of pride and boasting were attached to one's origins and what political leader or religious ancestry one could be traced back to. Who was your founder? Well, Paul was affirming that God had founded the church, and the political ruler was Christ. Moreover, the foundation was upon (not "for") good works. In other words, there is a proper foundation for the people created. How and why a people were created was just as important as their present, and certainly their future. In many cases, the future of the people is directed by their past. So, the founding principles are critical; Paul was affirming precisely this for the church.

Now once again, we see that Paul was indicating that the goal or purpose of God's actions was to form us as his workmanship so we would walk in these good works. This same verb "walk" had been used in 2:2 to describe how we used to walk in sin; now, in Christ, we are called to walk differently. You see, God always had a plan for how we should be humans and live in the world (see 1:4–5). We were created for doing good and being a blessing to others. Christ lived out this plan; he demonstrated how it could be done. He is our example, our ideal Ruler. He is our Messiah and King; he is the Head of the body. So then, 2:10 is Paul's crystal clear statement of God's plan to found a people in Christ Jesus to live after his example in the world.

1. What problem was Paul confronting when writing 2:8–10?

2. What has God made believers to be? Why has he created the church the way he has?

3. How should we live now?

WEEK THREE

GATHERING DISCUSSION OUTLINE

A. Open session in prayer.

B. View video for this week's readings.

C. What general impressions and thoughts do you have after considering the video, readings, and the daily writings on these Scriptures?

D. Discuss questions based on the daily readings.

    1. **KEY OBSERVATION**: People are influenced to live disobediently from a variety of sources: social, political, and spiritual. Often these are quite integrated; thus, it is sometimes difficult to sort out what we are following. Bad influences will promote disobedience to God. But we should understand where sinful living leads: death.

    DISCUSSION QUESTION: What positive and negative appeals are commonly seen in advertisements? Do these threaten our living for God?

    2. **KEY OBSERVATION**: Jews and Gentiles are alike in their dilemma: both sin and experience death. In fact, sin runs very deep and gets embedded in our bodies, will, and reasoning. As a consequence, we become "children of wrath" (Eph. 2:3).

    DISCUSSION QUESTION: Where does sin reside in people? How does it manifest itself?

3. **KEY OBSERVATION**: God responds to our deadly sinfulness with rich love and mercy. Specifically, God made us alive with Christ, raised us up with him, and seated us with him in the heavenly realms.

    DISCUSSION QUESTION: How and why has God shown sinful humans his mercy?

4. **KEY OBSERVATION**: God's plan is a long-term one for humanity. It is salvation that comes from his grace. This grace must be met by us with trusting faith in God's provision of Christ as our sacrifice. The way that God has planned salvation ensures that no one person has any boast over another.

    DISCUSSION QUESTION: How important is it that Paul explained in detail the source of our salvation? Why?

5. **KEY OBSERVATION**: Ephesians 2:8–10 are the thesis statement for the letter. Paul was stating positively what God had provided and created in Christ Jesus while also making statements to counter perennial social-political perspectives that set people against people. Boasting was a problem. Rather, what Paul set forth is that the church is God's creation, founded upon the good works of Jesus Christ; thus, the church should live accordingly.

    DISCUSSION QUESTION: What has God made believers to be? Why has he created the church the way he has?

E. What facts and information presented in the commentary portion of the lesson help you understand the weekly Scripture?

F. Close session with prayer.

WEEK FOUR

Ephesians 2:11–22

The Peace of Christ for Jew and Gentile as One Body

INTRODUCTION

After providing a broad overview of God's purposes in the world now and in the future to address the problem of human sin by being merciful in Christ Jesus, Paul continued his letter to the Ephesians by describing how Christ has overcome the hatred that existed between the Jews and non-Jews, that is, the Gentiles or nations. Paul built his statements up to a thesis statement in 2:8–10. Then, 2:11–22 formally begins Paul's development of the theme of 2:8–9—explaining the origins of God's salvation in Christ and the lack of any basis for boasting among the Jews. The development of the theme of 2:10— God's founding of the church body in Christ to live in good deeds—is taken up in chapters 4–6 and presents a counter political reality to what people saw and experienced in the Greco-Roman world.

Here in 2:11–22, Paul addressed the hatred between Jew and Gentile and how this has been overcome by Christ. Historically in covenant with God, the Jewish nation had been called apart from the nations to be separated from them. God's plan all along was that the Jewish nation would be a blessing to all the nations and be a light for them. However, after centuries of strife and conflict with the nations, it is not surprising that God's people began hating the nations, who already hated Israel. This awful situation is what God sent Jesus into, to unify both parties into a new humanity. Moreover, this new humanity was to be metaphorically a temple place, a space where God dwells. Thus, Paul described all believers together as the temple of God. What this means is that all parties now have equal access to God; the implication is that any other temple space is rendered obsolete.

ONE

Remember the Alienation

Ephesians 2:11–12 *So then, remember that at one time you Gentiles by birth, called "the uncircumcision" by those who are called "the circumcision"—a physical circumcision made in the flesh by human hands—*[12]*remember that you were at that time without Christ, being aliens from the commonwealth of Israel, and strangers to the covenants of promise, having no hope and without God in the world.*

Understanding the Word. We see the name-calling right away. Paul asked the Gentiles to recall their former state. They were called "the uncircumcision" by the Jews, who were called "the circumcision." You may or may not know what circumcision is: it's the removal of the foreskin around the glans of the male penis. This practice dates back to Abraham and God's requirement of all his male descendants and slaves to undergo circumcision. Why God called Abraham and the Israelites to perform circumcision is difficult to fully understand; it may have been to communicate a profound awareness that male aggressive sexuality was to be kept in check since circumcision rendered their male organ as belonging to God. Also in Scripture, circumcision was a metaphor for having a holy and transformed heart and hence a "circumcised" heart (Deut. 10:16; Jer. 4:4). Some medical reasons may exist also; circumcised males are less prone to infections, but it is uncertain whether this played any part in God's mandate. However, the effect of circumcision was to separate Jew from non-Jew in appearance. This caused conflict both ways, and increasingly during the centuries leading up to Christ. Jews were ridiculed and persecuted because of their circumcision. In athletic contests and at public male baths, their circumcision could be seen. This caused some Jewish males to undergo a very painful process to reverse the circumcision, called *epispasm*. All this explains why labeling people as "circumcised" or not mattered so much: circumcision was a symbol of belonging to God's people.

So here we see Paul asking the Gentiles to remember this animosity. Name-calling is never a good state of affairs. Notice how quick Paul was to indicate that circumcision is "made in the flesh by human hands." This qualification became important, because as he continued to explain how the Gentiles are now fully accepted by God, he showed that they are made into God's temple "in the Spirit" (2:22 NKJV).

In 2:12, Paul provided a list of what the Gentiles had once lacked: they were (1) without *Christ*, (2) being aliens from the *commonwealth of Israel*, (3) and strangers to the *covenants of promise*, (4) having no *hope*, and (5) without *God* in the world. This is quite an interesting list, because it is prioritized starting with Christ, the Jewish Messiah, and builds climactically to God. The second item on the list speaks to the political alienation from the commonwealth of Israel. Gentiles had no share in this reality. Also, they were considered "strangers to the [Jewish] covenants of promise." Because of this, they really had no hope and in the end were "without God in the world." This is a terrible way to live. However, this list was written from a Jewish perspective; it does not reflect God's perspective as revealed in Scripture. God had always set his mind on the nations, and now they were included in the gospel of Christ. In fact, as Paul will show in 2:13–22, each of these five deficiencies is now available to the nations when they become believers in Jesus Christ.

1. Why was circumcision important for the Jews?

2. What resulted from the Jewish religious and national zeal in regard to relating to the nations?

3. What were the Gentiles lacking from a Jewish perspective? Why were these significant?

TWO

Once Far, Now Near by the Blood of Christ

Ephesians 2:13–14 *But now in Christ Jesus you who once were far off have been brought near by the blood of Christ. ¹⁴For he is our peace; in his flesh he has* *made both groups into one and has broken down the dividing wall, that is, the hostility between us.*

Understanding the Word. We begin to see Paul's turnaround here. The "But" indicates a contrast, as does the word "now." He was saying, "You were once like this, but now you are like this." What made the difference? What allowed the change of status? "In Christ Jesus" and "by the blood of Christ." Jesus makes all the difference. Throw Jesus into the mix, and things look different.

Paul here spoke in terms of time and physical space: once far off, now brought near. This language is from a prophecy in Isaiah 57:19 that Paul will explicitly quote four verses later in Ephesians 2:17. Isaiah was envisioning a restoration of God's people and the restoring of peace. Paul understood this peace to involve Gentiles being brought near alongside the Jews. But how is this peace possible? Christ is our peace: this is a social-political peace with deep religious roots. Christ stands between Jew and non-Jew and brings them together through his sacrifice. This is amazing. Jesus was rejected by both Jews and non-Jews equally. All of humanity rejected Jesus, and Jesus was crucified. However, the early Christians understood this as a sacrifice, and they got this idea from Jesus himself. Jesus likened his body and his blood to a Passover lamb—that is what Christians celebrate at the Lord's Table, Communion, or the Eucharist—these are different names for remembering Christ's life and death by eating the bread and the wine that represent Jesus' body and blood. By Jesus' "flesh," that is, his actual body as an offering to God, Jesus "made both groups into one." He unified all of humanity in his act of dying on the cross.

Jesus effectively stood in the middle of the two opposing human forces—Jews and Gentiles—and took the blows they were throwing at each other. He forgave them at their worst. On a mission trip once, our youth group was playing a game of ultimate Frisbee. Two good friends were on opposite teams—they were massive young men who played football. At one point there was a contested call, and these friends were face-to-face, about to exchange punches. Right when they started, another friend of both of them, rushed in between them, and as they were punching, this third friend was also getting hit. Eventually, he was able to push them away from each other, and they came to their senses. This friend acted as Jesus did. Jesus stood in the middle between the Romans (the Gentiles) and the Jewish authorities. The Gospel accounts explain the different political maneuvering and scheming at Jesus' "trial," which was really no trial; it was a travesty of justice, the worst of the best of humanity. The Romans and the Jews each could lay claim to boasting rights—but with Jesus' crucifixion both were unmasked and shown to be no different, no better than the other. Jesus has a way of doing that—equalizing the playing field.

Paul's description of the brokenness of humanity uses the metaphor of a "dividing wall." Although scholars will debate what this refers to, it was a common political metaphor at a minimum—we erect walls to separate ourselves from others. Also, it is likely a reference to the wall that existed around the Jewish temple area, to separate the Gentiles from getting close to the temple. In fact, at each entry point, there was a sign warning the foreigner that he would be responsible for his own ensuing death if he passed the wall. Jesus destroyed that wall.

1. What does it mean to be far from God? What does it mean to be near?

2. How did Jesus unify Jews and Gentiles? What implications does that have for us today?

3. What walls do we set up to separate ourselves from others? How would Jesus take those walls down?

THREE

Christ Makes Peace

Ephesians 2:15–16 *He has abolished the law with its commandments and ordinances, that he might create in himself one new humanity in place of the two, thus making peace, [16]and might reconcile both groups to God in one body through the cross, thus putting to death that hostility through it.*

Understanding the Word. The core of the Jewish covenant with God was the Law, which contained specific commandments; this law of Moses identified and unified the people of God as well as separated them from the surrounding nations. Many of the commandments might seem strange to us, such as the prohibiting the eating of this or that, and so forth. However, these commandments were often directed to prevent the Israelites from worshiping idols and false gods. For Israel, the Law was a prized possession. It is "holy, righteous and good" (Rom. 7:12 NIV). The problem with the Law is not the Law itself, but the people trying to live under the Law—the Law never removes our problem with sin; it only identifies sin in us. Paul explained in Galatians that the Law was given to God's people as a provisional measure, like a school tutor with a child. The tutor is very valuable, teaching and training the child. However, the child needs to grow up and become a functioning adult. The tutor is no longer needed, although many of the principles, disciplines, and capacities fostered by the tutor will be seen in the life of the adult. The goal, argued Paul in Galatians 3:23–27, is Christ. The Law as a tutor leads us to Christ.

This is why when Christ came, he made peace by abolishing (or annulling) the Law, with its commandments and ordinances. The word "ordinances" here always refers to human-made laws (as opposed to God's commands). What happened with the Law over time was that it was supplemented with human additions in an attempt to follow the Law completely. The problem, however, is that these human additions began to detract from the real focus and center of the Law itself. People in their eagerness and attempt to keep the Law were actually moving away from the central ideas. Jesus confronted this among his contemporary Jewish teachers (see Matthew 15:1–14). It happens. We get distracted; in our best attempts, we miss out on the truly good. Our best attempts, too, may be attempts to hide our sinfulness; we often want to justify ourselves.

Jesus, however, saves us from ourselves and our best attempts that may end up alienating others. Jesus annulled the Law, with its ordinances, in order to "create in himself one new humanity . . . thus making peace." This is quite a statement. Paul was simply explaining in different ways what he had been affirming already: Christ is our peace and unifies enemies into one body, one new humanity. He does this through dying on the cross.

The sign of the cross of Christ is a helpful symbol because it points upward vertically and outward horizontally. Paul had been stressing the horizontal— that is, human to human—peacemaking unification of humanity. It is reconciliation between enemies. However, even more fundamentally, the cross of Christ points us upward, showing us the reconciliation humans receive with God. Reconciliation is more than forgiveness; I might forgive someone and he or she never be reconciled with me. That may be that individual's choice. However, reconciliation means being restored into proper, good relationship with the other. God reconciles us by the cross of Jesus; but we need to participate in this restoration. We receive forgiveness from God, forgive one another, and then live lives that reflect reconciliation: restored relationships in which hostility is put to an end.

1. Why was the Law given to God's people? What are the ordinances mentioned here?

2. How and why has Christ made peace? What implications does this have for our lives?

3. What is reconciliation in the gospel of Christ? How is this related to forgiveness?

FOUR

Opened Access

Ephesians 2:17–18 *So he came and proclaimed peace to you who were far off and peace to those who were near; ¹⁸for through him both of us have access in one Spirit to the Father.*

Understanding the Word. Paul knew something about Jesus historically: Jesus came seeking and saving that which was lost (see Luke 19:10). He came seeking people, even people who were far away. The parable of the prodigal son well illustrates this; if you are unfamiliar with the parable, you may want to read it now (see Luke 15:11–32). Jesus proclaimed the good news to both the Jews and the non-Jews, even though the Jews had some priority, since they were the historic people of God. Paul himself reflected this pattern when he wrote, "I am not ashamed of the gospel; it is the power of God for salvation to everyone who has faith, to the Jew first and also to the Greek" (Rom. 1:16). The point is that all people are loved by God even though God chose to reveal himself historically in a special way to one people group, those from Abraham's descendants. God had to start somewhere, and began with them. However, God's vision was always to reach all the nations. Jesus shared in that vision; he understood it; that is why he healed the Syrophoenician woman's daughter (see Mark 7:24–30) and the Roman centurion's servant (see Luke 7:1–11),

43

and conversed with and saved the Samaritan woman (see John 4). Jesus was fulfilling the mission of God.

Ultimately, what was at stake was our equal access to God. "Through [Christ] both of us have access in one Spirit to the Father." Wow. This is the bottom line, really. No more exclusive claims to God. No more denouncing others. We should recognize here also the presence of each member of the Trinity: Jesus, the Spirit, and the Father. We should recall that Paul asked the Gentile readers to remember that once they were without Christ and without God in the world (see Ephesians 2:12). Now, however, they have God in full: Father, Son, and Holy Spirit.

Here the Spirit's role is emphasized as the means to gain access. What kind of access? The term here implies that the person approaching has gained suitable status. What status? That of a son or daughter; family status. We each gain direct access to God the Father in the one Spirit. Hopefully, you have had a good experience with an earthly father or mother. But if not, the Holy Spirit will help you approach God as Father; we are privileged to enjoy this relationship of caring and affirmation!

It is important, too, to notice that the Spirit is identified as the one Spirit. In the ancient world, this was a helpful qualifier, since there were many spirits roaming around. People would attempt to access and control these different spirits, or to be controlled by them in some form of divination. It could get quite confusing. Paul in his letters addressed the Spirit's role in worship as "the same Spirit" that works in and through believers to serve and encourage one another (see esp. 1 Corinthians 12). We don't each have our own spirit that we use or manipulate as we like; we each share in the one Spirit, and this fact will affect how we relate to one another. Later, in Ephesians 4:3, Paul will emphasize once again the Spirit's role to bring unity and peace. No one has more access than any other; we all through the same, one Spirit gain access to the Father.

1. To whom did Jesus preach the good news, and why?

2. What does it mean to have access to God the Father? How do you experience this?

3. What is the significance of the one Spirit granting us access to the Father?

FIVE

The Temple of God—His People

Ephesians 2:19–22 *So then you are no longer strangers and aliens, but you are [fellow] citizens with the saints and also members of the household of God, ²⁰built upon the foundation of the apostles and prophets, with Christ Jesus himself as the cornerstone. ²¹In him the whole structure is joined together and grows into a holy temple in the Lord; ²²in whom you also are built together spiritually [literally, in the Spirit] into a dwelling place for God.*

Understanding the Word. What is the most precious place to you? What makes it so special? How often do you get to spend time there?

God's favorite place is with his people. He enjoyed walking with Adam and Eve in the garden of Eden. He enjoys our company too; he made us, after all. Historically, God has allowed a centralized place for people to come and worship him at his tabernacle and later in his temples. There have been two temples. This physical location unified people, and allowed the Israelites a space and time to learn about God. God was slowly revealing more and more about himself. The temple was a sacred place, a special place; however, God also needed to teach his people that the temple was not to be trifled with; when the people of God rejected him, so also did God reject the temple. God was more than a temple dweller; he is bigger than that. He did not need a temple, but was simply accommodating us as humans, who like special, sacred places. Human religions often have such temple places, holy sites, and shrines. We like them; it helps define where God is. The problem is that God is bigger than we think. Also, God loves all people more than we think.

God has taken great measures to restore us into fellowship with him, to reconcile us back to him. Jesus is the key. Jesus ended the alienation and allows us no longer to be "strangers and aliens" but rather "citizens." The terms used here are political in nature; just as once the Gentiles were "aliens from the commonwealth of Israel" (Eph. 2:12), now that former political status is fulfilled in believers becoming fellow "citizens with the saints," that is, God's people. We now can become full members of God's household; we have a place to belong. This is why we can call each other brothers and sisters. This is no trite statement; it is our new reality.

45

But more than this, Jesus' sacrifice of himself initiated the formation of a new structure of life, a new sacred space, a new temple place: humans themselves. Of course, in Jesus God fully dwelled. Jesus was a full human being, and God inhabited him. Jesus himself was a walking temple, bringing God's presence to people! Thus, Jesus opened the way for all people to be the place where God dwells. This occurs individually for each one of us and corporately for us as a body of believers. We together are the temple of God. This must have been mind-blowing for the earliest believers, since they saw temples all over. Now they were walking and talking temples.

While Paul was speaking metaphorically to some extent, there were tremendous implications for believers living on the ground in Ephesus. It was wrong for them now to go into the temples and participate in pagan worship. What replacement for this existed? Well, they had no need for a physical temple space; God resides in each one and among all believers. We are well-connected to God: we all have the Father, the Son, and the Spirit dwelling within us.

1. What is your most precious place? Where do you experience God?

2. Why do humans need temples? Does God need a temple?

3. In what ways are believers the temple of God?

WEEK FOUR

GATHERING DISCUSSION OUTLINE

A. Open session in prayer.

B. View video for this week's readings.

C. What general impressions and thoughts do you have after considering the video, readings, and the daily writings on these Scriptures?

D. Discuss questions based on the daily readings.

1. **KEY OBSERVATION**: The Jew and Gentile relationship was quite a strained one in the time of Christ. It resulted in labeling people on the basis of the practice—or nonpractice—of circumcision. Also, the Jews believed the Gentiles to be lacking several significant things; they were deficient not least with regard to Christ and God. The good news is, however, that God believed differently about the nations.

   DISCUSSION QUESTION: What were the Gentiles lacking from a Jewish perspective? Why were these things significant?

2. **KEY OBSERVATION**: Jesus makes all the difference to bring people together. He did so by becoming our peace in a comprehensive way; historically, this involved his dying at the hands of Jewish and Roman authorities as representatives of the human race. All of us are guilty for killing the guiltless One. Jesus died as a sacrifice for each of us, forgiving us all at that very moment. God's best meets the human worst. Metaphorically, Jesus took down the dividing wall of hostility between people.

DISCUSSION QUESTION: How did Jesus unify Jews and Gentiles? What implications does that have for us today?

3. **KEY OBSERVATION**: Jesus abolished the Law, with its commandments and ordinances, in order to bring humanity together. He made peace, and now Jew and Gentile have become a new humanity. Jesus brings about reconciliation not only between humans but also with God.

   DISCUSSION QUESTION: What is reconciliation in the gospel of Christ? How is this related to forgiveness?

4. **KEY OBSERVATION**: In the gospel of Jesus Christ, all people now gain access by one Spirit to God the Father. This was Jesus' mission, to reach all people and share this access with them.

   DISCUSSION QUESTION: What does it mean to have access to God the Father? How do you experience this?

5. **KEY OBSERVATION**: Humans like temples, and God historically worked through physical temple places. However, Jesus Christ brings God's presence to us; he is a walking temple. When we believe in Christ, we are transformed from aliens into fellow citizens of the saints; we are now household members, brothers and sisters. We are built into a temple place where God dwells.

   DISCUSSION QUESTION: Why do humans need temples? Does God need a temple?

E. What facts and information presented in the commentary portion of the lesson help you understand the weekly Scripture?

F. Close session with prayer.

WEEK FIVE

Ephesians 3:1–13

Paul's Suffering, God's Grace, and the Gospel Proclamation

INTRODUCTION

How would you feel if your pastor or mentor got hurt, especially because they had helped you? Paul was imprisoned on behalf of the believers at Ephesus. What seems to have prompted Paul's imprisonment this time was his traveling to Jerusalem to deliver a financial gift that his churches had raised for the needy Christians there. At the Jewish temple, Jews from the Ephesus area accused Paul of speaking against his people, the Law, and the temple itself. As a consequence, Paul was eventually imprisoned and taken away from Jerusalem, probably never to return again. While in prison, he wrote Ephesians.

Paul suffered and was imprisoned as a result of his preaching the good news of Jesus and bringing Jew and Gentile together in Christ. However, he did not want believers to take this badly. He was fulfilling the call of God to make known God's plan: Jews and Gentiles were now reconciled into one body. The Gentiles were included in God's saving purposes and now have an inheritance in the future. The gospel, in fact, revealed God's plan, which actually showcased God's multifaceted wisdom to human rulers and the authorities in the heavenly realms.

For the task given to Paul, God supplied him with abundant grace. Paul experienced this grace as a power inside of him to preach the gospel and spread the word to as many people as possible. Therefore, Paul urged the Ephesians not to lose heart at his suffering; God had his back.

ONE

Paul's Backstory, Part I

Ephesians 3:1–4 *This is the reason that I Paul am a prisoner for Christ Jesus for the sake of you Gentiles—²for surely you have already heard of the commission of God's grace that was given me for you, ³and how the mystery was made known to me by revelation, as I wrote above in a few words, ⁴a reading of which will enable you to perceive my understanding of the mystery of Christ.*

Understanding the Word. Paul was imprisoned several times. In this instance, he was arrested on the false claim of having brought a Gentile into the Jewish temple. Also, the Jews from the area of Ephesus charged him with speaking against the Jewish people, the Law, and the temple (see Acts 21:27–28). Paul's letter to the Ephesians addressed these claims, especially the previous section, in 2:11–22. That is why Paul here at 3:1 says, "This is the reason that I Paul am a prisoner." What happened was that Paul attempted to defend himself at Jerusalem, but due to the anger against him, he was taken away by the Roman authorities. When they learned of a plot to kill Paul, he was escorted away with 470 Roman soldiers and brought to Caesarea Maritima for two years while they figured out what to do with him. Meeting with several high-ranking Roman and Jewish officials there, eventually Paul had to appeal to higher justice, the emperor, and was then taken to Rome (for details, see Acts 21–26).

Paul wasn't caught off guard. He was expecting to suffer while proclaiming the gospel. Jesus predicted that his followers would not be popular, and even persecuted when proclaiming the gospel. In fact, when the Lord called him, he said of Paul, "he is an instrument whom I have chosen to bring my name before Gentiles and kings and before the people of Israel; I myself will show him how much he must suffer for the sake of my name" (Acts 9:15–16). So, Paul knew that he would suffer.

However, more important than his suffering was the grace that God showed him. Paul often talked about this grace. He didn't tire of it. Notice from today's passage that grace is given for the benefit of others: "God's grace . . . was given me for you." We shouldn't just wallow in the grace, as great as it is. Grace is meant to be experienced and shared. If you have received grace, share that with others. God's grace is infectious, and we all need it.

In Ephesians, we are privy to experiencing Paul's grace, because he wrote about it! What Paul was writing down was an outflow of the grace of God. Paul was given particular insight into the nature of God's purpose and will. This is called the "mystery." Despite our use of the term (and the meaning in the ancient world), the Christian mystery is meant to be made known. In Ephesus and elsewhere, there were mystery cults and groups that formed around these cults. They reenacted the founding of the cult. We don't know much about these cults, because the knowledge was hidden from outsiders under penalty of curses. The initiates into the cults were not supposed to share the initiation rites. Not so with the mystery of Christ! Christ is to be proclaimed. Moreover, Paul wrote down his understanding of the mystery of Christ so the Ephesians could read it again (and again and again). Now we are reading about it too. We may need to read it again and again because Paul's writings are quite profound and sometimes hard to understand (see 2 Peter 3:15–16).

1. Why was Paul arrested? How does Ephesians address the circumstances of his arrest?

2. How have you experienced God's grace? How would this be appropriate to share with others?

3. What was the mystery given to Paul?

TWO

This Is the Mystery: Gentiles Are Fully Included in God's People!

Ephesians 3:5–6 *In former generations this mystery was not made known to humankind, as it has now been revealed to his holy apostles and prophets by the Spirit: ⁶that is, the Gentiles have become fellow heirs, members of the same body, and sharers in the promise in Christ Jesus through the gospel.*

Understanding the Word. The mystery of Christ receives greater explanation here. We learn that earlier generations of God's people didn't know it. What might Paul have meant by this? Didn't God predict the coming of the

Messiah in the Old Testament, especially in the Prophets? Well, yes and no. God certainly did, and yet it was not the clearest to the Jewish people. One section of Isaiah is particularly relevant, Isaiah 40–55, which describes a figure called the Suffering Servant. What made this difficult to understand was who this person was, because surely the Messiah wouldn't be rejected, suffer, and die. This didn't fit the bill. Also, Isaiah's vision included benefits for the Gentile nations. No, the Jewish people wanted—no, deserved—a strong Messiah who would do battle with the nations and restore glory to God by destroying them. So, as Jewish scholars studied and looked at their Scripture, it was hard for them to discern the fullness of the Messiah and what he would look like. The Jewish Messiah was not supposed to be a suffering one who would extend benefits to the nations. This explains why Peter tried to oppose Jesus after he revealed his need to die. Who wants to be a disciple of a suffering Messiah? This explains why Paul said, "this mystery was not made known to humankind, as it has now been revealed to his holy apostles and prophets by the Spirit."

Jesus himself and his Holy Spirit (given to believers after Jesus had ascended to God's right hand) helped the first disciples, and especially their leaders, the apostles and prophets, to delve more deeply into the Scriptures and understand God's purposes: the suffering Messiah would bring benefits to those near (Jews) and those far away (the Gentiles). Indeed, the suffering part of Jesus' life was a stumbling block for many Jews and simply foolishness to the Gentiles (see 1 Corinthians 1:23). But Paul explained that Christ's suffering death was an acceptable sacrifice to God, and was done in such a way as to show both Jews and Gentiles their need.

More to the point here, in fact, the Messiah Jesus unified both groups into one body. In particular, what Paul stressed is the inclusion of the Gentiles into God's people. Again, I cannot emphasize enough how significant this is; before this message, the Jews and the Gentiles were literally at each other's throats. So, Paul underscored the Gentile inclusion by providing a list. He walked around the topic by drawing upon different aspects of the same thing. He looked at it from various angles. The Gentiles are "fellow heirs" of the glorious future that God has in store for his people. They are "members of the same body," which implies a unified political entity under the headship of Christ the Lord. And they are "sharers in the promise in Christ Jesus through the gospel." Here the promise would include the giving of the promised Holy Spirit. If you read the book of Acts, you discover that the giving of the Spirit is a very significant event, not only for the first believers at Pentecost and potentially for the Jews hearing the first sermon by Peter (see Acts 2:33), but also for the first Gentile converts. In fact, the reception of the Holy Spirit when they believed sealed the deal for the Jews observing: "All the circumcised believers who came with Peter were amazed, because the gift of the Holy Spirit had been poured out on the Gentiles also" (Acts 10:45 NASB). The Gentile believers are legit!

1. Why was the mystery of Christ not so easily understood by former generations?

2. What role does the Spirit play in the mystery of Christ?

3. In what ways are Gentiles included among God's people? Are they on equal status?

THREE

Paul's Backstory, Part II

Ephesians 3:7–9 RSV *Of this gospel I was made a minister according to the gift of God's grace which was given me by the working of his power. ⁸To me, though I am the very least of all the saints, this grace was given, to preach to the Gentiles the unsearchable riches of Christ, ⁹and to make all men see what is the plan of the mystery hidden for ages in God who created all things . . .*

Understanding the Word. The gospel is truly good news. That's what the word means. It is the best thing happening on the planet, and off-planet. As we have learned, the gospel brings peace between enemies at a horizontal level and a vertical level. Think of the directions of the cross. At the horizontal level the reconciliation is between types of people who are wildly different: the Jews and the Gentile nations. There was no way that these two could ever be brought together in an equal marriage, so to speak, not without a radical change and conversion of one or the other. Any Gentile would have to be converted to Judaism, meaning painful circumcision as the initiation rite for any male. In God's wisdom, however, a different way was conceived in which the two groups were wedded together, a way in which each party was not subsumed by the other. This was a sensitive proposal, and the first years of the marriage were rocky ones. Someone needed to provide firm, loving, and scriptural marriage counseling. That counselor was the apostle Paul, who wrote letters helping people understand the new marriage of Jew and Gentile in Christ.

Paul's pedigree in many ways reflected the best of both worlds. In terms of Judaism, he excelled and surpassed his peers in his eagerness and commitment to the Jewish customs (see Galatians 1:12–24; Acts 26:4–5). In terms of the Gentiles, Paul was a Roman citizen and was raised in Tarsus, a university town in eastern Asia Minor. Tarsus was renowned for its education in philosophy and rhetoric; two famous Stoic philosophers came from there (Zeno of Tarsus and Chrysippus). Paul may have learned the fundamentals of rhetoric there, even though he received a Jewish education in Jerusalem under the famous teacher Gamaliel. In the book of Acts, Paul explained this interesting mixture when preparing for and giving a speech to Jews in Jerusalem: "I am a Jew of Tarsus in Cilicia, a citizen of no insignificant city" (21:39 NASB) and "I am a Jew, born in Tarsus of Cilicia, but brought up in this city, educated under Gamaliel, strictly according to the law of our fathers, being zealous for God just as you all are today" (22:3 NASB).

So God set apart Paul to be a minister by grace. The word "minister" is the basis for the church office of deacon. However, Paul was not referring to this later church position here, but was describing his role as an intermediary agent for Christ. The word signified an assistant to a superior carrying out the tasks of that superior. Paul was a servant of the gospel, a gospel that proclaimed the mystery of Christ revealed to unify Jew and Gentile together in Christ. Being a servant to such a gospel meant that Paul had to suffer a lot; the marriage of Jew and Gentile in this way had a very rocky start. Jewish teachers and missionaries tried to thwart Paul and taught that new Gentile converts needed to be circumcised. Paul argued against this (see his letter to the Galatians). On the other side, the Gentile governing authorities were puzzled because Paul seemed to be proclaiming a rival Lord to Caesar; Paul was disrupting the social-political system. Caught between both sides, Paul took on more and more the life and suffering of Christ. Hence, Paul relied on God's gift of grace "by the working of [God's] power" to sustain him.

1. What is the meaning of the word "gospel," and how are Jew and Gentile united by it?

2. What prepared Paul to be a servant of the gospel?

3. How was Paul a servant of the gospel?

FOUR

God's Wisdom on Full Display

Ephesians 3:10–11 NIV *His intent was that now, through the church, the manifold wisdom of God should be made known to the rulers and authorities in the heavenly realms, [11]according to his eternal purpose that he accomplished in Christ Jesus our Lord.*

Understanding the Word. God's purposes are to reveal himself and his plans for maximum saving benefit for humanity. God does not force himself on us; we might want him to do so. We might want him to be more glorious, more obvious, more evident in what he is doing. However, God is working for a salvation from the inside out. He works within the system of humans to effect a powerful and complete transformation. This is the plan of God, or what Paul called God's manifold wisdom. God's plan involves humans being changed and acting courageously within the world's structures to effect change and bring illumination, to save people and change hearts, one person at a time. As we are transformed to seek to save others, we ourselves undergo salvation. As we participate in God's purpose as Christ's church body, we experience more and more God's salvation. Sin runs deep; God's salvation runs deeper still to the very heart of the matter.

God is working to undo sin at multiple levels of reality simultaneously. We often are quite preoccupied with sin within us. This certainly should concern us, although for me focusing exclusively on my own sin issues has had only benefits to a limit. This makes sense, since by focusing primarily on myself, I am only seeing part of the problem, in isolation from a broader context. So, I have grown the most in my struggle with sin by looking outward, by looking to God, his provision, his grace, his power, and by then doing what I ought to be doing, seeking the salvation of others. If I fill my life with doing good, then what room is left for doing bad?

In 3:10, Paul explained that God's manifold wisdom (that is, his multi-faceted plan of salvation) is revealed to the human rulers and to the spiritual authorities in the heavenly realms through the church body. At higher levels of human political organization, and even spiritual oversight, the church body displays God's wisdom brilliantly. How so? Well, first, as Paul explained, the church joins together two people groups at great odds with one another: Jews and Gentiles. To human rulers, the church body is the place where peace can be found. Any other human basis is secondary, if not even faulty.

Likewise, formerly the Jews and the Gentiles had their own god(s) overseeing them; their respective deities were worshiped with equal zeal. However, now both groups are brought together in Christ under the auspices of the one true God. This gospel gives testimony to the heavenly authorities, that is, wayward spiritual beings, that God is God, and they are not! Their days of wreaking havoc, causing confusion, and fostering fear by deceiving people into worshiping what they should not are over. Although believers are not to dwell on such entities, it is clear that they exist. Most peoples across the world know that these lesser divinities are there; they assign many names to them and are often cowed into trying to appease them. But Christ is seated above them and we are with Christ, and so we have no reason to fear them. Instead, our fear and reverence are directed to God. As we will see, Paul will argue that believers struggle against human rulers and spiritual powers in the heavenly realm by wearing God's armor (see Ephesians 6:10–20).

1. How is God's manifold wisdom seen in the world?

2. How deep does human sin go? How deep does God's salvation go?

3. Why would God reveal his wisdom to the rulers and the authorities in the heavenly world?

FIVE

Not Being Discouraged at Sufferings

Ephesians 3:12–13 **NIV** *In him and through faith in him we may approach God with freedom and confidence.* *¹³I ask you, therefore, not to be discouraged because of my sufferings for you, which are your glory.*

Understanding the Word. We feel bad when someone working for us gets hurt. Could you imagine how the first believers felt about the apostle Paul being imprisoned for serving them? Paul really did not want them to be discouraged or to lose heart because of this. He thus asked that they would not. Instead, Paul said that his sufferings reflect their glory. How? Well, God and Paul valued their salvation so much: if Paul's suffering would bring their salvation, then, he said, "Bring it on!"

It may be helpful to set before you the extent of Paul's suffering as he recounted them in his letters. He provided lists of such hardships in 2 Corinthians, written two years before Ephesians. Why Paul had to explain this to the Corinthian believers is a long story! Basically, the Corinthians thought that Paul's suffering was an embarrassment and only showed that he did not have God's approval; anyone suffering so much must be a bad person! We sometimes have the same attitude. We must be careful or else we may find ourselves in the place of Job's friends, not understanding suffering and simply being present with those who do suffer. (See the Old Testament book of Job.) God does not promise to prevent suffering in this life; he promises to be present, to strengthen, and to help us as we suffer. Paul affirmed that "we may approach God with freedom and confidence"; God hears us; we can be brutally honest, like Paul.

> But we have this treasure in earthen vessels, so that the surpassing greatness of the power will be of God and not from ourselves; we are afflicted in every way, but not crushed; perplexed, but not despairing; persecuted, but not forsaken; struck down, but not destroyed; always carrying about in the body the dying of Jesus, so that the life of Jesus also may be manifested in our body. For we who live are constantly being delivered over to death for Jesus' sake, so that the life of Jesus also may be manifested in our mortal flesh. So death works in us, but life in you. (2 Cor. 4:7–12 NASB)

> but in everything [we are] commending ourselves as servants of God, in much endurance, in afflictions, in hardships, in distresses, in beatings, in imprisonments, in tumults, in labors, in sleeplessness, in hunger, in purity, in knowledge, in patience, in kindness, in the Holy Spirit, in genuine love, in the word of truth, in the power of God; by the weapons of righteousness for the right hand and the left, by glory and dishonor, by evil report and good report; regarded

as deceivers and yet true; as unknown yet well-known, as dying yet behold, we live; as punished yet not put to death, as sorrowful yet always rejoicing, as poor yet making many rich, as having nothing yet possessing all things. (2 Cor. 6:4–10 NASB)

1. In what way can believers approach God? Why is this important?

2. How do you view suffering? Does the gospel of Christ bring a different view of suffering?

3. In these lists, what can you learn of Paul's response to suffering? What motivated Paul?

WEEK FIVE

GATHERING DISCUSSION OUTLINE

A. Open session in prayer.

B. View video for this week's readings.

C. What general impressions and thoughts do you have after considering the video, readings, and the daily writings on these Scriptures?

D. Discuss questions based on the daily readings.

1. **KEY OBSERVATION**: Paul knew suffering. He expected it, because God had told him and others that he would suffer. More important than this, however, was God's grace to empower Paul despite his sufferings, to share his understanding of the mystery of Christ to others. The Letter of Paul to the Ephesians is an outpouring of the grace given to Paul. We experience grace as we read about it.

   DISCUSSION QUESTION: How have you experienced God's grace? How would this be appropriate to share with others?

2. **KEY OBSERVATION**: The mystery of Christ was hidden from former generations. Even though elements of the suffering Messiah and extending of blessings to the nations are seen in Scripture, it was difficult to accept the reality of the King of Israel suffering a terrible death and benefiting the Gentiles. But the Spirit reveals the truth. Christ's death and resurrection brought Jew and Gentile together so that Gentiles included into God's people share the same benefits.

   DISCUSSION QUESTION: What role does the Spirit play in the mystery of Christ?

3. **KEY OBSERVATION**: Paul was given the task as a minister to preach the gospel. His educational background allowed him insight into Jewish and Gentile thought. He needed much grace in the form of power to perform this task, since he received heavy opposition. However, God's grace in the form of power was not given so that Paul could dominate others, but so he could persist in pointing others to Christ through enduring hardship and to enable him to continue to serve even as he suffered.

   DISCUSSION QUESTION: What prepared Paul to be a servant of the gospel?

4. **KEY OBSERVATION**: God's purposes of salvation give testimony to human rulers and spiritual authorities in the heavenly realms. Specifically, the church body is God's instrument to reveal this multi-faceted wisdom.

   DISCUSSION QUESTION: Why would God reveal his wisdom to the rulers and the authorities in the heavenly world?

5. **KEY OBSERVATION**: We can approach God about any and every subject, even our suffering. Although suffering is unpleasant, God does not promise that we will escape suffering, but he brings perspective and hope in the midst of it. Paul asked believers not to lose heart at his sufferings; in fact, he said, they "are your glory." Better yet, Gentiles' salvation by being incorporated into Christ's body is even more glorious!

   DISCUSSION QUESTION: How do you view suffering? Does the gospel of Christ bring a different view of suffering?

E. What facts and information presented in the commentary portion of the lesson help you understand the weekly scripture?

F. Close session with prayer.

WEEK SIX

Ephesians 3:14–21

Paul's Prayer for Power to Comprehend God's Love

INTRODUCTION

In 3:14–21, we see Paul once again take a posture of prayer. Already Paul had prayed for the believers in 1:15–23. Many interpreters have noted strong similarities of content between the two prayers: God's revelation, knowledge, love, and a vision of God's power manifested in Christ. People repeat what is most important to them. So, Paul reiterated some important points as a way to summarize what he had been writing to the Ephesian believers.

In these verses, we visibly observe Paul bowing down to God as the Father of all fathers. God is the source of all, and so Paul confidently prayed for a host of deeply penetrating things for believers. As Paul prayed, he revealed more and more about what is possible for people. He expands our vision; he enlarges our view of God and our place in God's plan in Christ. The possibilities are endless.

ONE

Bowing down to the Father

Ephesians 3:14–15 NASB *For this reason I bow my knees before the Father,* *15from whom every family in heaven and on earth derives its name, . . .*

Understanding the Word. Because of all that Paul had been writing, he adopted a posture of prayer: "For this reason I bow my knees before the Father." However, this posture is distinctive. Jews would adopt various positions for prayer, but more typically standing (see, e.g., Mark 11:25; Luke 18:11). However, bowing one's knee is appropriate for someone approaching a mighty king, a royal figure. Such a posture of petition places the prayer within a specific context. Paul's kneeling makes sense in view of the political vision of God's purpose to form a unified, new humanity around Jesus Christ our Lord. Paul's posture is like the prophet Daniel's, who, in defiance to the Babylonian king, did not bow to him, but rather bowed down to God to pray. For Daniel, the bowing of the knee communicated his resistance to human claims to ultimate rule. When King Darius signed the decree for the people in his kingdom not to pray to any god or human, Daniel deliberately and defiantly bowed his knees three times a day in prayer to God (see Daniel 6:8–10).

Paul found himself in a similar situation: he had been arrested by the governing authorities and was awaiting trial as a political prisoner. He was caught between the Jewish authorities and the Roman ones, not unlike Jesus. Acts 23–26 records the names of the important people with whom Paul met: the Jewish ruling body (the Sanhedrin); Herod's Praetorian Guard; the governor Felix and his wife, Drusilla; Felix's successor, Porcius Festus; the high priest, Annas; the powerful lawyer Tertullus; the commander Lysias; the Jewish king Agrippa and his wife, Bernice; and the Caesar Nero. Paul did not bow down to them, but Paul defended himself saying, "I have committed no offense either against the Law of the Jews or against the temple or against Caesar" (Acts 25:8 NASB). And he testified to King Agrippa, "I did not prove disobedient to the heavenly vision, but *kept* declaring both to those of Damascus first, and *also* at Jerusalem and *then* throughout all the region of Judea, and *even* to the Gentiles, that they should repent and turn to God, performing deeds appropriate to repentance. For this reason *some* Jews seized me in the temple and tried to put me to death" (Acts 26:19–21 NASB).

Paul bowed down to God as the Father from whom every family or fatherhood derived its name. In the underlying Greek, one sees an important word play: Father (*pater*) and fatherhood (*patria*). God's fatherhood is being stressed here and across Ephesians. More than any other letter of Paul, Ephesians identifies God as Father (eight times). Why? Well, we must remember the God folder that Paul was concerned to fill. God as Father would have evoked various images in the minds of his audience. Among Jews the understanding of God as Father was common (e.g., Deuteronomy 32:6; 1 Chronicles 29:10 NASB; Isaiah 63:16; 64:8). However, among the general Gentile populace, "Father God" would have signified Zeus (Greek) or Jupiter (Roman). The philosopher Epictetus (AD 55–135) wrote a long treatise in which one section is devoted to explaining how life principles may be derived "from the principle of God being the father of all [people]."[1] Also it is intriguing that the emperors at this time enjoyed the special title *Pater Patriae* "Father of the Fatherland" that was frequently found on coins. Paul effectively subordinated all claims of fatherhood to God, even the most powerful humans are subordinate to God.

1. What was conveyed as Paul bowed his knees when praying to God the Father?

2. What was Paul's response when facing the most powerful people in the world?

3. Why is God being Father so significant?

T W O

Praying for Strength Inside

Ephesians 3:16 NASB *[I pray] that He would grant you, according to the riches of His glory, to be strengthened with power through His Spirit in the inner man, . . .*

Understanding the Word. In 3:16 we begin to see the content of Paul's prayers. Essentially, it is for the believers "to be strengthened." However, Paul added several important qualifiers that we should seek to understand. First, Paul prayed for this in view of the abundance of God. He asked that the giving of strength be out of and corresponding to "the riches of [God's] glory." We have seen Paul stress both God's wealth and God's glory. There

---

1. Epictetus, *The Discourses of Epictetus, with the Encheridion and Fragments*, trans. George Long (London: George Bell and Sons, 1890).

is no shortage of either for God. God has all resources available to him. He is rich in grace through Christ Jesus both offered in the forgiveness that we can receive (see 1:7), but also in terms of favor to be displayed in the coming ages in kindness (see 2:7); he is rich in the glorious inheritance that he offers believers (see 1:18); and he is rich in offering us mercy when we are most in need of it (see 2:4). Also, God is the Father of glory (see 1:17); we offer up praise to God's glory as a response to all that God has done for us (see 1:12, 14); we offer up praise for the glory of God's grace as shown in Christ the beloved One (see 1:6). God's glory refers to God's being and nature as revealed to his people. His glory is synonymous with his renown and awesomeness, which describe who God is. What Paul was saying here is that God's glory is revealed in the gospel of Jesus. Paul himself had experienced this glory, and it is out of the wealth of God's glory that he prayed for others to be strengthened. Importantly, as believers are strengthened, they are able to reflect God's glory back into life and the world.

The next two qualifiers are in the phrases "with power through His Spirit." This seems quite redundant: "to be strengthened with power." However, Paul in Ephesians repeated and piled up Greek words for power. He did this for impact and to underscore the importance of power: 1:19 has four words; 3:7 has two; 3:16 has two; 3:20 has two; 6:10 has three. It's worth considering how important power is for living. In our own time, people seek for power and ability to do things. We aspire to great and greater positions of power and influence. We want to be effective. We like output and performance. We want to be energized and to feel strong. The range of meanings expressed here corresponds to the range of meanings in the Greek words used throughout Ephesians. In the ancient world, people were also attracted to power, and sought ways to religiously gain power. People recognized power as coming from the divine. In fact, whenever something powerful happened, it was thought to reflect the divine. Sometimes an altar or temple was erected right there on the spot! What Paul was saying to believers is that they are connected to the best source of power in the universe: God's Spirit. Throughout Paul's writings, it is clear that one role of the Holy Spirit is to mediate God's power. This is important, because this keeps power in the context of our relationship with God. It is not just random power, or power from any spirit, but it is power connected with God and God's mission. The Holy Spirit was given to continue the ministry of Jesus among believers.

Finally, the location of this Holy Spirit-given power is "in the inner man," or person. The importance of this will be discussed on Day Three.

1. What is God's glory?

2. What does it mean to be strengthened with power?

3. How does the Holy Spirit strengthen believers? Why?

THREE

Christ Dwelling in Our Hearts

Ephesians 3:17a NASB *so that Christ may dwell in your hearts through faith . . .*

Understanding the Word. On Day Two, we looked at the different qualifiers for the strengthening for which Paul prayed for believers. The last modifier was "in the inner man," or person (3:16 NASB). The power of God manifest to us is an internal power. This is a power to think right, have the right attitudes, to be strong in resolve, and to live differently in the world. As much as we might like to have external power—power to lift things, fly through the air, perform amazing feats (hence, our culture's gravitation toward superheroes)—we have been given something to help our souls: power inside of us.

But why exactly did Paul pray the way he did for us to be strengthened? Well, the purpose of such strengthening is found in 3:17a: "so that Christ may dwell in [our] hearts through faith." The verb "dwell" means to take up sanctuary, as in a temple. We are walking temples, and every temple has its god. Why is such power through the Holy Spirit so needed that Christ must dwell in our hearts? I think the answer is quite simply that we have a lot of junk to move out of our hearts. It takes a powerful moving team to clean up house.

Our hearts are complex things. They reflect our deepest self. Out of our hearts our longings emerge. We store things in our hearts, which in turn direct our hopes and dreams. Too often, because of the hurts that we all experience, our hearts may become wounded; we stop hoping and dreaming and longing for what is better. We become preoccupied, busy, and even sometimes hopeless and despondent. All of this comes from our precious hearts.

Humans are permeable creatures. We are subject to influences. We are meant to be filled with God. But when we walked away from God, we became filled with other things, which begin to influence our desires and will and life-styles for the worse (see 2:1–3). In the absence of God, we may be filled with ourselves and quite self-preoccupied and self-absorbed. Instead of this, we need to have faith in God.

When accused of being the king of evil spirits because he was casting out demons, Jesus told a parable about a person who has had an evil spirit removed (see Luke 11:20–26). The spirit returns to find the person like a house "swept and put in order." Then it goes and finds seven other spirits more evil than itself, and they come back to the person, and his final condition is worse than before. Although Jesus was not describing the pattern for each person and how it always happens, he was making an important point. It is not enough to get rid of the bad influence or spirit and clean our own house and put it in order: we must be filled with the right Spirit. That Spirit is Christ. Christ was made to be in our hearts and our hearts were designed to receive Christ. This was God's plan from the beginning—to be so close to us as to be on the inside, not forcefully, but relationally. Evil spiritual influences actually enslave people, make them addicted to things, and dehumanize them. Christ frees us. As Paul said, "For freedom Christ has set us free" (Gal. 5:1). It is actually quite natural for us to have Christ dwell in us, since he himself was a human being and was filled with the Holy Spirit. Likewise, we believers are filled with Christ in the Holy Spirit for fellowship with God. We have the Trinity of God in us through faith.

1. Why is it necessary to be strengthened in the inner person?

2. What does "dwell" mean? What does it mean that Christ dwells in our hearts?

3. What evil spiritual influences struggle for a place in your heart?

FOUR

To Know Christ's Love, Which Surpasses Knowledge

Ephesians 3:17b–19 NASB . . . and *that you, being rooted and grounded in love, *[18]*may be able to comprehend with all the saints what is the breadth and length and height and depth, *[19]*and to know the love of Christ which surpasses knowledge, that you may be filled up to all the fullness of God.*

Understanding the Word. Understanding 3:17b–19 is difficult, because Paul has continued piling on idea after idea. Some interpreters may take this as another item for which Paul was praying, as the NASB translation may imply by saying: "*and* that you . . ." However, it is better to understand these verses as another level of why Paul was praying, the purpose behind it. Visually, we can track the logic of Paul's prayer like a cascading waterfall:

Paul prayed that

3:16 God would grant power in the inner person through the Holy Spirit,

3:17a in order that Christ would dwell in our hearts through faith

3:17b–19a in order that we would comprehend . . .

3:19b in order that we would be filled with God.

Each "in order that" reflects a further purpose or reason why Paul prayed the way he did. Whenever you can discern the purpose for a person's actions, often it clarifies those actions. Here we could also work backward from the final or ultimate goal and retrace the steps. Paul's ultimate reason for praying the way he did was so that believers would "be filled up [with] all the fullness of God." We are vessels of God's presence; this only makes sense in light of what Paul has already argued: believers are the temple of the living God. That is a big space to live into; it takes prayer. So, as we track backward, we observe the steps that go into this final goal.

In order to be filled with God, we need comprehension and knowledge (3:17b–19a). Of what? Well, "the love of Christ," essentially. There is a problem, however. Paul explained that this love "surpasses knowledge." If so, then how are we to know the love of Christ? I think it is a lot like loving a spouse. I have a wife, and to really know her surpasses knowledge. I could not simply write a

67

book about her and convey the knowledge logically or in some other systematic way. Our relationship transcends raw knowledge because it is a relational knowledge. Paul was speaking here to relational knowledge of Christ's love; it cannot fully be known until it is experienced. How? In what way or dimension can it be experienced? Paul described this love in terms of "the breadth and length and height and depth." Scholars have wondered why Paul used these dimensions here to describe Christ's love. The dimensions may speak to the profundity of the love—it is beyond mathematical computation, so to speak, yet occupies all space. More likely, however, Christ's love was being likened to an altar space where sacrifices were made. The prophet Ezekiel used these four dimensions to describe the altar of sacrifice in the new temple to be formed for God's people, which God's glory fills (see Ezekial 43:13–17). We have already observed that Paul likened believers to a temple and that Christ will dwell in their hearts. This is an amazing prayer, like none other in the Bible. As you can see, believers are full of God (3:19b), Christ (3:17), and the Holy Spirit (3:16).

1. What was Paul's ultimate goal for praying here?

2. How does one comprehend and know the love of Christ?

3. What does Christ's love allow believers to be full of?

FIVE

God Is Glorified in the Church through God's Ability to Work in Us

Ephesians 3:20–21 NASB *Now to Him who is able to do far more abundantly beyond all that we ask or think, according to the power that works within us,* [21]*to Him* be *the glory in the church and in Christ Jesus to all generations forever and ever. Amen.*

Understanding the Word. It is quite fitting for Paul to end the wonderful and climactic prayer in 3:16–19 by giving glory to God. In 3:20–21 Paul concluded with a doxology; a doxology literally is "a word of praise." May God receive glory! Already we have seen that God is glorious; here Paul stressed that the church and Christ are vital agents for God to be glorified. It is quite notable that the church is placed first in the word order; that's just how important the church is. Remember that the church is Christ's body.

The English translation struggles to convey the exuberant wording of this doxology in the Greek text behind it. The English expression "far more abundantly beyond" is really one long word in the Greek, an adverb. It is the king of adverbs! In Greek, typically adverbs are shorter words that pack an important punch. But this word is the longest adverb in the New Testament and is made with fourteen letters! God is the One able to do far more abundantly beyond everything we ask or can conceive. In theory, we probably know this to be true. This is by definition what God is—all-powerful. But Paul placed a very specific and important qualification here: "according to the power that works within us." Paul wanted us to see that we are the location of God's amazing ability to act. This action is within us. This may make us feel uncomfortable, because we can more safely think about God working outside of us. He can do amazing things in very general ways; he can orchestrate events in miraculous ways that only he can do; he can work through the hands of doctors and even beyond doctors to heal and restore life and wholeness; he can bring supplies to needy people quite surprisingly and just in the nick of time; he can encourage people. I have seen these things and can testify to them.

Although Paul's focus was squarely on God's ability, we must see, however, that Paul was also focusing on "the power that works within us." Us. Paul's point seems to be that there may be a potential weakness in God's power working; that problem is us. We may not be asking enough or even conceiving enough what God can really do and accomplish through us. This may make us feel uncomfortable, and yet in many ways God wants to work great things through us. Paul's life provides perhaps the most poignant example of someone being delivered from his sinful self and hurtful experiences and going on to do great things. Despite opposition to his message, he persisted. Despite persecution and suffering, Paul was encouraged to continue on. It is really important to consider that Paul probably had in mind our human life capacities and courage to live for God in the midst of conflict: God is able to do far more than we ask or even consider in the midst of our life circumstances. Sure, we should think big; but we should be cautious about avoiding responsibility at the scale that we can act. Remember that God wants to bring salvation within the system, and through us. He wants to work in and through us, and that requires us to grow up, to be re-equipped in our thinking about what's important, and then to act courageously in love; God's power is working within us. Again, we are not necessarily going to be airlifted from our situation; but God will supply us with grace and love and power to be in the situations in which we find ourselves in such a way as to bring light, love, forgiveness, and reconciliation—and these things take much power to see through. This is why Paul included "the church" and even placed it before "in Christ Jesus" as the place where God is glorified.

1. How is God glorified on earth?

2. What does it mean that God can do more abundantly than we ask or think?

3. What role do people have in bringing glory to God?

WEEK SIX

GATHERING DISCUSSION OUTLINE

A. Open session in prayer.

B. View video for this week's readings.

C. What general impressions and thoughts do you have after considering the video, readings, and the daily writings on these Scriptures?

D. Discuss questions based on the daily readings.

1. **KEY OBSERVATION**: In the face of human opposition and the most powerful people in the world, Paul stayed true to God's calling and gave testimony to the gospel. Even in prison, Paul bowed his knees to the One he knew was the most powerful person in the world, God the Father.

   DISCUSSION QUESTION: What was Paul's response when facing the most powerful people in the world?

2. **KEY OBSERVATION**: Paul prayed that believers would be strengthened with power. This comes from the Holy Spirit and has as its destination our hearts.

   DISCUSSION QUESTION: How does the Holy Spirit strengthen believers? Why?

3. **KEY OBSERVATION**: Believers are strengthened in order to make room for Christ to dwell in our hearts. Our hearts are precious places—in

fact, sacred places, like a temple. Our hearts were made to have God dwell within them; Christ is the natural fit, being God in human form.

DISCUSSION QUESTION: Why is it necessary to be strengthened in the inner person?

4. **KEY OBSERVATION**: Paul ultimately prayed in order that believers would be filled with the fullness of God. Steps along the way require the work of the Holy Spirit in the inner person, Christ dwelling in our hearts through faith, and comprehending the love of Christ. Indeed, believers are the temple of God and filled completely with God through Christ's love.

   DISCUSSION QUESTION: How does one comprehend and know the love of Christ?

5. **KEY OBSERVATION**: Paul concluded his prayer with a doxology. He first, however, identified God as able to do more than we ask or can conceive. In doing so, Paul wanted believers to understand their role alongside Christ to bring glory to God.

   DISCUSSION QUESTION: What does it mean that God can do more abundantly than we ask or think?

E. What facts and information presented in the commentary portion of the lesson help you understand the weekly Scripture?

F. Close session with prayer.

WEEK SEVEN

Ephesians 4:1–16

The Calling, Gifted Leaders, and Purposes of the Body of Christ

INTRODUCTION

Having described Christ's sacrificial work to bring peace and unify Jew and Greek in one body politic and Paul's own sacrificial work in preaching and praying for the church, Paul turns now to describe more and more what this new political entity, the church, looks like. What are its fundamental premises? What truly unifies it? What are its marching orders?

These final three chapters of Ephesians are organized around the verb translated "to live," which literally means "to walk." (English translations will typically use one or the other: *live* or *walk*.) Paul used this verb strategically in 2:1–2 to describe a negative walking ("you were dead in your sins, in which you once walked/lived," paraphrased) and then positively in 2:10 ("We are God's workmanship, founded in Christ Jesus upon good works, which God prepared in advanced, in order that we would walk/live in them," paraphrased). As I have explained, in 2:10 Paul was providing the thesis statement for these last three chapters, which repeat this verb "walk"/"live" five times. In each instance, the verb begins a new train of thought or unit. These units provide a road map for us as we continue reading through Ephesians:

4:1–16 Walking Worthily of the Calling in the Unity of the Faith
4:17–32 Not Walking like the Nations, but Learning Christ
5:1–7 Walking in Love, Imitating God in Christ
5:8–14 Walking in the Light, not Darkness, and Producing Fruit
5:15–6:9 Walking Wisely and Being Filled with the Spirit

Paul then concluded climactically in 6:10–20 by calling God's people to arms to resist evil agents by donning the armor of God. But we are getting ahead of ourselves. So, let's focus on how Paul would have us now live.

ONE

Social Virtues of the Faith

Ephesians 4:1–3 ESV *I therefore, a prisoner for the Lord, urge you to walk in a manner worthy of the calling to which you have been called, ²with all humility and gentleness, with patience, bearing with one another in love, ³eager to maintain the unity of the Spirit in the bond of peace.*

Understanding the Word. Although a prisoner for the Lord Jesus Christ, Paul was in a strong position to encourage believers to live differently in the world. He had undergone a radical transformation in his own life from being a persecutor of Christ-followers to being their biggest cheerleader. Even from prison, Paul urged us on to live differently in the world.

In 4:1–3, Paul laid some important groundwork. He placed an important framework around the Christian life: God's gracious calling. Really, all of 1:3–3:21 has been describing the gracious, merciful, loving actions of God as God's calling. God wants all people to be saved (see 1 Timothy 2:4) and calls all people to be a part of the family. The word for "calling" means "invitation"; it's like being invited to participate in an important event, a dress-up event. People need to come dressed properly when invited. If they don't dress properly, then they truly haven't understood the invitation properly; they have received the wrong call, so to speak. It's embarrassing to show up to an invitation-only event underdressed. So, our response to God's invitation should correspond with the call itself: we must walk worthily of that calling. What sort of response is worthy?

Paul described social virtues by providing a list. You might think of it as a checklist to respond to the invitation. Every time you see a list (there are many in the latter half of Ephesians), you should carefully consider the relationship of the elements to one another. How do they relate? Is there a movement or buildup to something important? Is there an inner-to-outer movement? In this list, there is a movement from one's inner disposition (humility and gentleness) to one's treatment of others (patience, forbearance, love), and finally to a preemptive, larger concern for unity in the body (eagerness, bonding). These are virtues that allow us to live together in unity. Let's look more carefully at them.

Humility is an interesting term; in Jewish culture, it was a positive virtue, but not so in Greek culture. It must have been a bit challenging for the believers in Ephesus for Paul to begin with this virtue, since it was typically an attitude expected of a servant; it carries a sense of non-assertiveness. Paul stressed it by adding the qualifier "all." Gentleness refers to sensitive, careful treatment of others. For example, in Galatians 6:1, Paul advised the spiritually mature believers to restore one caught in sin with "a spirit of gentleness."

Patience concerns long-suffering; we work with people in a way that does not rush them. The word "[for]bearing" means putting up with obstinate, objectionable, or even antagonistic behavior (see Acts 18:14; 1 Corinthians 4:12; 2 Corinthians 11:1, 4, 19–20; 2 Thessalonians 1:4) and may even require forgiveness (see Colossians 3:13). There is a presumption here that believers in community will have to forbear each other's "issues" and even sin. This is rather sobering; the church is not made up of perfect people, but people in need of forgiveness; we are all in process. Love is absolutely central to Paul's Christian ethic in his letters, and in Ephesians in particular; love is exemplified by Christ's love and self-sacrifice (see 5:2; cf. 3:17–19).

Finally, Paul urged an attitude of eagerness. We don't often use this word, but it is a positive characteristic. In particular, believers here work with the Spirit, who also promotes unity.

1. What is God's calling? How comprehensive is it?

2. What do each of these virtues listed by Paul mean? Which virtue captures your attention?

3. What prevents unity in the body of Christ?

TWO

The Unified Foundation for Believers

Ephesians 4:4–6 ESV *There is one body and one Spirit—just as you were called to the one hope of your call—*⁵*one Lord, one faith, one baptism,* ⁶*one God and Father of all, who is over all and through all and in all.*

Understanding the Word. The fast pace of our lives distracts us from having a single purpose and unifying center. In many respects, this is quite unavoidable with all our commitments, relationships, goals, and projects. It is a rat race. Alternatively, some people are so purposeless that they fill their lives with meaningless activities, diversions, and entertainments—even addictions. Some people seek chemical highs; some seek activity highs. What unifies us? What is worth bringing us together into a meaningful and healthy center?

Paul here provided the absolute foundation for the church. There are seven "ones." The number seven is significant in Scripture because it represents perfection and completeness. Oneness implicitly denotes exclusivity; if there is one God and Father, there is no other. Despite the claims that there are many lords and many gods, Paul argued, "yet for us there is one God, the Father, from whom are all things and for whom we exist, and one Lord, Jesus Christ, through whom are all things and through whom we exist" (1 Cor. 8:6).

Additionally, this list of seven elements is quite important for several reasons. First, we see the Trinity present: God in three persons—Father, Son, and Spirit. We would expect God to be our foundation, or center. Second, remarkably the church body makes the list. That is how important the church is. There is one body—not multiple bodies. Although there may be several individual congregations, we are one body of Christ. Christ unifies us as his body. We belong to one another, and no person is isolated or alone. Third, there are also, remarkably, three additional ones: one hope, one faith, and one baptism. Why would these be included in the list?

Baptism is the initiation into the body. As such, it represents an introduction into God and God's purposes and all the rights, privileges, and obligations thereof. It's that important. But does this refer to our water baptism or our

Spirit baptism? Yes. But if we need to prioritize, the list of ones appears to be arranged to place one baptism in relation to the one Spirit.

One faith and one hope in the list is intriguing. Among the various deities and cults established by the Roman people were Faith (Fides) and Hope (Spes). Faith for them carried the idea of "fidelity" and "confidence" in relationships, basically keeping good faith with one another. Hope was a central message of the Augustan emperors; hope represented their provision of prosperity for people within the Roman Empire. Coins were minted depicting both of the goddesses Spes and Fides. So, it appears Paul was resisting common Roman conceptions in their messaging of the importance of their empire; however, for believers, there is only one faith and one hope.

Finally, the list is arranged to place the Lord Jesus in the center as the fourth element; this properly stresses the centrality of Christ to bring unity. Paul had been stressing this. At the same time, the list builds to end climactically affirming the "one God and Father of all, who is over all and through all and in all." This flourish stresses God's transcendent, creative, and sustaining power.

1. What brings unity to your life?

2. How would this list have called believers to reorient their lives? How does it call us to do so?

3. What is stressed in the arrangement of the list?

THREE

Distributed Grace from Christ's Triumph

Ephesians 4:7–10 ESV *But grace was given to each one of us according to the measure of Christ's gift. [8]Therefore it says, "When he ascended on high he led a host of captives, and he gave gifts to men." [9](In saying, "He ascended," what does it mean but that he had also descended into the lower regions, the earth? [10]He who descended is the one who also ascended far above all the heavens, that he might fill all things.)*

Understanding the Word. Do you ever feel lost in the shuffle? Do you feel overlooked or insignificant? It is not all that uncommon to feel left out, benched, and not in the game. It sucks. The good news is that each one of us is a player in the game; each one of us matters. Not a little. But a lot. The church may seem to function as a lumbering mammoth, but it is composed of individuals. Each plays a pivotal part.

In the sentence word order of 4:7, Paul placed great stress on "each one" as a distinctive recipient of God's grace. This is not unique to Ephesians; Paul singled out individuals in Romans 12:3–5 and 1 Corinthians 12:7–11, which are passages that also explain the nature of God's grace and giftedness. This is where Paul was heading in Ephesians 4:11–12 when he listed leadership gifts to help God's people perform ministry work. Before this, however, Paul announced a victory.

In 4:8, Paul quoted from the Old Testament a passage that originally was praising God for his victory to save his people, those in captivity (see Psalm 68:18). This is what happened in wars. People got captured by the enemy when that enemy seized territory. Although the psalmist was referring to the people of God scattered when the first temple was destroyed and the people were taken into captivity, Paul expanded the vision in several significant ways. First, Christ is the one acting as the Victor; the "he" refers to Christ. Originally, the psalm spoke of "you," referring to God. If Christ is the victor, who might the enemy be that had taken territory and its captives? Presumably, the evil one, Satan. Paul did not specify this, and we need to be careful not to read too much into things here, but each of us was a captive of the enemy, alienated from Christ. He won us back; he paid the ransom to set us free. Another significant change of Psalm 68:18 is the flow of the gifts. Here is the first part of Psalm 68:18:

> You have ascended on high, You have led captive *Your* captives;
> You have received gifts among men. (NASB)

Originally, we can see in Psalm 68:18 that God received the gifts from people. However, Paul updated the triumphal notion by showing that Christ gave gifts to people. This corresponded to the Roman military victories in which the conqueror (typically a Roman general, but then only the emperors) first received the bounty of spoils in the war and then gave gifts to the soldiers. Paul was presenting a counter-victory, one that rivaled Roman victories. Such a view gains further support because Paul in 4:9–10 explained Christ's ascending as implying his descent first. Christ first came down to earth to gain the victory before rising (from the dead) and ascending to God's right hand. What makes this so interesting is that the Romans believed their rulers to be quasi-gods coming down to earth and then dying and going back in spirit; but they were not resurrected. So, Paul quoted, updated, and interpreted Psalm 68:18 in light of God's victory in Christ; in so doing, Paul was lifting up Christ for believers to cherish as the Victor surpassing imperial victories. Christ frees us and gives us gifts.

1. Are you a spectator or a player in the game? What are you enabled to do for God's glory?

2. How did Paul interpret and update God's victory in Psalm 68:18? Why did he do so?

3. How did Christ achieve his victory?

FOUR

Gifted Leadership for Good Purposes

Ephesians 4:11–13 ESV *And he gave the apostles, the prophets, the evangelists, the shepherds and teachers, [12]to equip the saints for the work of ministry, for building up the body of Christ, [13]until we all attain to the unity of the faith and of the knowledge of the Son of God, to mature manhood, to the measure of the stature of the fullness of Christ, . . .*

Understanding the Word. On Day Three we looked at Christ's victory and his distribution of grace to each individual. What gifts did Christ give to people? Well, the interesting thing is that the gifts are people. Christ won people from the enemy—these are the spoils of war—and then gave these gifts to people. This is wonderful and shows us the amazing work of God to restore creation and rehabilitate people with people. We are God's instruments on earth. If we were sitting on the sidelines, he puts us back in the game. He saves us to deploy us strategically for his purposes, and each one of us plays a pivotal role in the battle. I recently visited the USS *Midway* aircraft carrier in San Diego. It was amazing. As we toured the massive ship, what began to strike me was how diversified the crew was. It was literally a miniature city, with mechanics, cooks, tailors, mail room clerks, doctors, dentists, prison guards, and on and on, all the way to the top commander. Each played an important role; each carried out specific tasks that, combined, were greater than the possible impact of any singular person, even as important as that person might have been.

Paul in 4:11 described gifted leaders. Although he had already affirmed in 4:7 that grace (and implicitly giftedness) is given to each individual person, here Paul was looking at the leaders of Christ's church body, and particularly those who speak: apostles, prophets, evangelists, shepherds, and teachers. Apostles are frontline evangelists who go to new places to win converts and plant churches. Some will maintain that the apostolic office was restricted to only those first disciples, who saw Jesus' earthly ministry and witnessed Christ resurrected; this view existed among the earliest followers of Jesus (see Acts 1:21–22). Such a definition put Paul in a precarious position, because he probably did not see Jesus before his crucifixion but saw Jesus in a vision; so Paul identified himself as "one [apostle] untimely born" (1 Cor. 15:8). But Paul elsewhere identified people as apostles who probably did not meet these requirements (see Romans 16:7). So, in the end, it is reasonable that missionary apostles who plant churches exist today. Prophets are those who interpret the Word of God and speak its truth to people. Evangelists are those who proclaim the truth of the gospel to people. Whereas apostles are frontline workers, evangelists will give witness in areas already reached. Shepherds are pastors, leaders who care for people and speak God's truth into their lives. Finally, teachers are those who study and explain the nitty-gritties of God's Word to people. They may systematize and expound the truths of God's Word.

What is the purpose of these ministry activities? Paul explained three purposes: (1) to equip the saints (God's people) for doing service; (2) to build up the body of Christ morally (encouragement) and numerically (adding members); and (3) to help the church attain to the unity of the faith in the knowledge of the Son of God, the perfect Man, the Christ, who is the mature example of what it means to be a human being. Christ sets the example for us;

he is the conquering General and sets the tone and mission of the body. These leadership roles in the church are important; pray for them!

1. What gifts did Paul focus on in 4:11–13? Why?

2. What is an apostle? Do apostles exist today?

3. What role do the leaders of the church play, and what purpose do they have?

FIVE

Maturity and Organic Growth in Love

Ephesians 4:14–16 ESV *so that we may no longer be children, tossed to and fro by the waves and carried about by every wind of doctrine, by human cunning, by craftiness in deceitful schemes. ¹⁵Rather, speaking the truth in love, we are to grow up in every way into him who is the head, into Christ, ¹⁶from whom the whole body, joined and held together by every joint with which it is equipped, when each part is working properly, makes the body grow so that it builds itself up in love.*

Understanding the Word. God's gifting of certain individuals for speaking and leadership is absolutely critical for the church. Why? Because these leaders set the tone and agenda for much of what God's people do. If the leaders of the church are not fulfilling their role, the church will suffer in its witness to God's saving activity in the world. Essentially the leaders are to point believers to Christ as the Son of God, the perfect person, and the example of maturity.

In 4:14–16 Paul elaborated these points by first showing what would happen if the leaders fail in their purpose in preparing people to serve and pointing people to Christ and then by positively showing the properly functioning church body. Let's take these in order.

Who likes adults who act like adolescents? The fact is, the emotional level of adults may be quite younger than their physical age; when faced with difficult circumstances, we may offer a twelve- or thirteen-year-old response. I feel that way sometimes. Those were hard years for many of us; do we really want to function emotionally like that? Do we want to stay like adolescents in our thinking? Why do people get stuck there? Well, I think there are several reasons: emotional and relational hurts that remain unforgiven; continued sinful living; and/or a lack of vision for life and a lack of an alternative goal. The leaders of the church help people mature as human beings to be functional and contributive to God's purposes in the world.

What are telltale signs of immaturity? Paul described a fickleness and a proneness to be carried about by different trends and viewpoints. This only makes sense; if there is no solid moral bearing, then people will be easily swayed to this or to that view. In general, American culture evidences these pendulum swings in terms of right or wrong. I would describe some now, except that a year or two from now, they would be different, and thus what I said would be dated. The sad thing is that Paul's description reveals that humans will prey on other humans. People will be "carried about . . . by human cunning, by craftiness in deceitful schemes." Rather than people being a blessing to other people as Christ's gifts, instead they prey upon others as means to their ends. We see this constantly. The human slave/sex trade is a global problem; pornography is the single largest online business, beating all other businesses combined. This is awful, humanity at its truly worst. It shows humans as infantile and abusive, not fulfilling their creative purposes but rejecting God's life. God weeps.

Positively, Paul showed that the church body is organic, made up of interlinking and interconnecting parts that help and build one another up as it grows into Christ its head. Amazing! What makes the whole process work is seen in 4:15: "speaking the truth in love." Truth sheds light in the midst of darkness; Paul will address this quite directly in 5:7–14 (see Week Nine). But truth without love fails to win over; and likewise love without truth is "sloppy *agape*" (*agape* is the Greek word meaning "love" here); people don't change. However, love in truth is really what makes the Christian life effective—valuing and seeing each other as God does. This is the true glue that Christ gives.

1. What happens if church leaders fail in promoting maturity in Christ? How do they fail?

2. What are telltale signs of immaturity? What are the most obvious examples that you see?

3. Describe the properly oiled and functioning church body. What is the most essential ingredient?

WEEK SEVEN

GATHERING DISCUSSION OUTLINE

A. Open session in prayer.

B. View video for this week's readings.

C. What general impressions and thoughts do you have after considering the video, readings, and the daily writings on these Scriptures?

D. Discuss questions based on the daily readings.

   1. **KEY OBSERVATION**: Like an invitation to a dress-up event, God calls people to be in the fellowship with Christ and the church. The invitation desires respect, and we should respond in a worthy manner to God's gracious, loving, and merciful invitation. The way we respond entails social virtues that allow believers to live in unity with one another: humility, gentleness, patience, forbearance, love, eagerness, and bonding.

   DISCUSSION QUESTION: What do each of these virtues listed by Paul mean? Which virtue captures your attention?

   2. **KEY OBSERVATION**: The foundation for believers for life is the oneness of central realities that includes the body, the Spirit, hope, the Lord, faith, baptism, and the God and Father of all. This list spoke to early believers and can also speak to our hectic and disoriented lives.

   DISCUSSION QUESTION: How would this list have called believers to reorient their lives? How does it call us to do so?

3. **KEY OBSERVATION**: Grace is distributed abundantly, reaching all people. What made this possible is Christ's triumph over the grave. Jesus fulfills God's role of rescuing God's people from the enemy. In the victory, Christ distributes the spoils of war to people.

   DISCUSSION QUESTION: How did Paul interpret and update God's victory in Psalm 68:18? Why did he do so?

4. **KEY OBSERVATION**: Christ gives people as gifts to people. Paul focused on leadership in the church in his letter here: apostles, prophets, evangelists, shepherds (pastors), and teachers. These roles collectively are to prepare God's people for ministry and to grow the church body together by focusing on Christ as the Son of God, the perfect person, and the example of human maturity.

   DISCUSSION QUESTION: What role do the leaders of the church play, and what purpose do they have?

5. **KEY OBSERVATION**: The goal that God has for humanity does not include immaturity, when people are prey to other people. Instead, God is working through Christ as the Head to have a functioning people that are truthful and loving and build one another up.

   DISCUSSION QUESTION: Describe the properly oiled and functioning church body. What is the most essential ingredient?

E. What facts and information presented in the commentary portion of the lesson help you understand the weekly Scripture?

F. Close session with prayer.

WEEK EIGHT

Ephesians 4:17–32

The Ethics of Learning Christ and Wearing the New Self

INTRODUCTION

In 4:17–32 we will look at the second walking section—remember that Paul organized the second half of his letter around the verb for "walk"/"live." These are some of my favorite verses in Ephesians. These verses contain some of the first direct commands. Although there have been implicit dos and don'ts previously, and 4:15 does contain an exhortation ("We must grow up . . . into Christ"), it is not as direct as the commands found in this week's passage. Paul really began to lay the hammer down and help move believers to a new life; here is where the rubber meets the road.

This section begins with a rather bleak depiction of fallen humanity in 4:17–19. It is a reminder that people are lost without Christ and are "alienated from the life of God." Then in 4:20–24 Paul speaks about learning Christ and reveals to us important details about early Christian teaching. It is moral-formative: put off the old self, be renewed in the disposition of your mind, and put on the new self, created according to God. This three-step process is seen elsewhere in Scripture. Then Paul gives ten new commandments in 4:25–32 that encourage putting off some old, bad behavior and putting on a self that is fitting with the redemption we have received.

ONE

How to Miss out on God's Life

Ephesians 4:17–19 NASB *So this I say, and affirm together with the Lord, that you walk no longer just as the Gentiles also walk, in the futility of their mind, 18being darkened in their understanding, excluded from the life of God because of the ignorance that is in them, because of the hardness of their heart; 19and they, having become callous, have given themselves over to sensuality for the practice of every kind of impurity with greediness.*

Understanding the Word. When Paul drew attention to his speaking, he meant business. When adults say to their children, "What I am saying is . . ." or "I am warning you . . ." they are trying to be real clear. Paul in 4:17 made reference to the act of communication "So this I say . . ." Furthermore, he also dropped the Lord into the mix: "and [I] affirm together with the Lord, . . ." These phrases increase the gravity of what Paul is about to say. They point forward and underscore their importance.

Paul urged believers to walk/live no longer like the Gentiles around them. This implies that believers in fact have a new identity. Remember in 2:11–22 that Paul indicated that Gentile believers had once been excluded from the commonwealth (citizenship) of Israel, but now they were brought near by Christ's sacrifice and had become cocitizens with the saints. Paul's strategy was to concisely describe the web of problems associated with unbelieving Gentiles. We need to track the implied logic of these listed items. One thing leads to another, and the final state is not pretty.

First, there is "the futility of [the] mind"; this refers to aimless and point-less focus of the mind's attention. People squander their minds. Why? Because they are "darkened in their understanding"; they have not been illuminated about God's plan for humanity through Jesus Christ. We should remember how Paul prayed for believers to have a spirit of wisdom and revelation in 1:17.

Second, they are "excluded from the life of God"; this is quite serious and actually incongruous. There is a sad paradox here, since people live and are sustained in material reality through God's sustaining power. God sustains his creation; humans are in fact dependent on the life that God allows them to have. Yet, Paul explained that they miss out on God's life. Why? Because of their ignorance—they don't know any better. This is why it is important to spread the gospel. This sheds light and helps people move from a place of ignorance to knowledge and hopefully then to trusting faith.

Third, they have "hardness of [the] heart"; this is a condition where one does not allow one's deepest self-openness to fellowship with God. Rather than a supple, pliant, and responsive heart, people can close themselves off and actually harden themselves from God's presence. However, God still seeks them out.

Fourth, such people, "having become callous" (that is, insensitive to right and wrong and God's attempts to reach them), "have given themselves over to sensuality." Devoid of God's presence and voice, people listen to their bodies and satisfy their cravings; they become preoccupied with what they feel and do what they want "for the practice of every kind of impurity with greediness." This last phrase can mean two things. The NIV 1984 version translated it as "with a continual lust for more." Sin never satisfies; it leaves one begging for more, addicted and not free. Alternatively, "with greediness" may reflect the greed and preying upon people that sin entails. Think of the worst sins committed and then track the money. People profit from sin; greed and sin go together.

1. How did Paul emphasize what he was about to say? Why?

2. What are some of the more striking things that Paul said about living apart from God?

3. What results when one is given to sensuality? Who benefits? Who loses?

TWO

Learning Christ and God's Three-Step Transformation Process

Ephesians 4:20–24 NASB *But you did not learn Christ in this way, *[21]*if indeed you have heard Him and have been taught in Him, just as truth is in Jesus, *[22]*that, in reference to your former manner of life, you lay aside the old self, which is being corrupted in accordance with the lusts of deceit, *[23]*and that you be renewed* *in the spirit of your mind,* ²⁴*and put on the new self, which in* the likeness of *God has been created in righteousness and holiness of the truth.*

Understanding the Word. Being a believer in Christ makes one a follower of Christ. Being a follower of Christ makes one a disciple and requires one to learn about Christ. Paul here called believers to recall what they had learned about Christ. Importantly, Paul said that believers "did not learn Christ in this way," referring back to the sinful life described previously in 4:17–19. This is a very important point; some people may believe that the more sinful they are, the more they can experience God's mercy, grace, and love. This is simply not true! We should not keep wallowing in sin, as if this may help us. Rather, Christ calls us out of sinful living.

What is particularly fascinating about 4:20 is that Paul used the verbal form for the word that is translated as "disciple" in the Gospels and the book of Acts. Oddly, this noun "disciple" is not found in the rest of the New Testament. However, we do find the verb form "to learn," as is seen here. The definition of a disciple is simply a "learner," one who learns through the instruction of another. So, a disciple of Christ learns Christ. Notice in 4:20–21 how many times Paul mentioned and referred to Jesus; how many times do you count? Paul wanted to stress the importance of Christ, and rightly so. He wanted believers to have the proper focus, to fill their minds with the right kinds of things, to pay attention to what matters in life and to the truth, since the "truth is in Jesus."

This last simple reference to Jesus alone is quite interesting; Paul added no other qualifiers, such as "Christ" or "Lord." This is somewhat unique. When Paul did refer only and simply to Jesus, he particularly had in mind the earthly life of Jesus as a real human being who lived, suffered, died, and of course, was raised to life again (see, for example, 2 Corinthians 4:10–12). It would seem that here Paul wanted us to ponder Jesus as a real human being; this recalls the Gospel accounts of Jesus. It is vital for us to read and reread the accounts of Jesus' earthly life and ministry in order to be his disciples and follow his example. The truth of being a human being is seen in Jesus' earthly life. What motivated Jesus? How did Jesus treat people? How did he minister to people? How did he confront and overcome evil? What did Jesus teach us through his words and example?

Now the content of learning Christ and being "taught in Him" is provided in 4:22–24. This is the real good stuff. Notice that this is a list, really, a three-step program. First, "lay aside the old self" involves a metaphor of undressing that is continued in 4:24 with dressing. Why do we take off the old self? Because it is corrupted by deceitful desires. Sin promises more than it can deliver. It lies. Second, "be renewed in the spirit of your mind." The verb tense here stresses the ongoingness of this renewing of the mind. We need always to fill ourselves with good thoughts (see Philippians 4:8–9). Garbage in, garbage out; godly thinking, godly living. Third, "put on the new self"; this new self is likened to God because we were made and remade in Christ in God's image. When we put on this new self, we will reflect and live "in righteousness and holiness of the truth." Remember that righteousness refers to living rightly with one another; holiness indicates purity. Both are informed by Jesus' truth.

1. What is the meaning of the word "disciple"? How is that meaning applicable here?

2. What was Paul stressing about Jesus?

3. What is God's three-step process of transformation in Christ? Where are you in the process?

THREE

Being Truthful

Ephesians 4:25–27 NASB *Therefore, laying aside falsehood,* SPEAK TRUTH EACH ONE *of you* WITH HIS NEIGHBOR, *for we are members of one another.* [26]BE ANGRY, AND *yet* DO NOT SIN; *do not let the sun go down on your anger,* [27]*and do not give the devil an opportunity.*

Understanding the Word. Paul continued in 4:25 with a "therefore" that logically connects what he will say next as a consequence of God's three-step process of transformation in Christ. If you recall that process, it involves (1) putting off something old and corrupted, (2) thinking in a renewed way, and (3) putting on the new self, created to be like God in right and holy living. This section then describes living anew as reflecting these three steps: don't do this, but rather this, because of this (thinking anew). Right thinking is so often the key to our right behaviors. Since ignorance was part of the problem, knowledge is part of the solution, knowledge of the truth.

The threefold pattern is found right away: put aside falsehood; put on truthful speaking, because we belong to one another. We saw earlier that "speaking the truth in love" is the means for the body of Christ to grow (4:15). Paul repeated this again. Truthfulness is that important. The truth is in Jesus. Paul also alluded to an Old Testament prophetic text when he said, "SPEAK TRUTH EACH ONE *of you* WITH HIS NEIGHBOR" (Zechariah 8:16: "Speak the truth to one another"). Where Paul alluded to or quoted Scripture, it is often instructive to look at the verse in its original context. Zechariah was calling for God's people to repent, return to God, and be restored to God. The first indication that Paul provided to reflect that repentance is this: "SPEAK TRUTH EACH ONE *of you* WITH HIS NEIGHBOR." Our truthfulness is the foundation for our new life in Christ. We should not lie to one another; we shouldn't deceive one another and take advantage of one another. Why? We are God's people and belong to one another. No one hurts without affecting others; no one benefits without affecting others.

One particularly hurtful thing we Christians do is hide our struggles from one another. We all come to church wearing our Sunday best, always smiling, even though driving on the way to the service, we were arguing and angry with each other and the kids. (Been there, done that!) Yet, this façade hides the reality of our struggle and sometimes even active sin in our lives. We do this to each other; we look better than we are. Facebook promotes this falseness too. When we are not truthful with one another, we may become envious and angry with ourselves and one another.

In 4:26 Paul turned to address anger. He once again alluded to Scripture—this time to Psalm 4:4 ("Be angry, and do not sin," [ESV]). This important psalm addresses how to handle it when people commit wrongs against you. We pray to God even as we are angry. But we do not retaliate; that is God's business. Indeed, if God is angered at our sin, why should we not be able to be angry also, especially if we are to be like God? However, our problem is that we may be misperceiving things and then act disproportionately to what actually happened. We don't know all; it's God's business to sort things out. So, while Paul allowed an initial response of anger, he very quickly added "yet do not sin." This makes all the difference. Moreover, Paul indicated that believers should not let the sun go down on their anger, which reflected wisdom expressed elsewhere at the time. The temptation is to stoke the fire of one's anger. We need to address it on the same day if possible; otherwise, we may be giving the devil an opportunity, literally, a "place," where he does not belong. We don't want to do that. The devil will use our anger against us and against others.

1. How important is truthfulness? How do we fail to be truthful to one another?

2. How honest should we be with one another?

3. When are you angered? How should we deal with our anger? Why?

FOUR

Doing and Speaking Good

Ephesians 4:28–29 NASB *He who steals must steal no longer; but rather he must labor, performing with his own hands what is good, so that he will have something to share with one who has need. 29Let no unwholesome word proceed from your mouth, but only such a word as is good for edification according to the need of the moment, so that it will give grace to those who hear.*

Understanding the Word. In 4:28–29 Paul continued the pattern of "don't do this, but do this," and then provided a purpose: "so that . . ." These two verses form the center of Paul's admonitions in 4:25–32; they are also important because of their content. Paul took up the classical pairing of word and deed. In our own language, we speak in such terms. Our words and actions reflect some of the most purposeful actions that humans perform with our mouths and hands. We are always working both parts of our bodies, and it is imperative that we control what we do and what we say very carefully. In fact, Paul placed both of these main human activities within the view of "good"; both our speech and our actions should be carried out with good in mind. Paul dealt with the *deed* first before moving to the *word*. Let's look more carefully at these.

Believers should not be stealers. In the ancient world, because there were limited goods—and because of the human tendency toward sinful laziness—people also developed a tendency to grab what they could. In Romans 2:22,

Paul accused his contemporary Jews of robbing temples. Acts 19:37 also mentions "temple robbers"—evidently this was a common enough practice that you could label people as such. Why do we steal? We think that we are gaining something, but ironically we are losing something: our character. Paul thus redirected the believers to work by using one's own hands to do "what is good." This places an important value on our work; humans are made to labor for the good. Notice that Paul provided a purpose for this good: "so that he will have *something* to share with one who has need." This is quite important, because it implies that not everyone will be able to work. Why? Old age, malady, injury, or some other bad circumstance. So, Paul urged people to work for the good of helping others who cannot work. How do we determine who can and cannot work? This is a touchy issue, but one always to be considered. In the early church, regulations were given for taking care of widows who were in need: see Acts 6:1–3 and 1 Timothy 5:3–16. In the latter passage, Paul articulated the need to distinguish widows truly in need from those not; he commanded younger widows to marry. In that culture, unmarried women had very limited opportunities, so marriage was the most honorable thing. In our own day, it is very exciting to learn that missionaries are helping people in need (women especially) to set up micro-businesses. God smiles upon this work; he needs more people to help with the harvest in the mission field.

Paul next urged good speech rather than spoiled breath. The word "unwholesome" literally means "spoiled," as in fruit. The metaphor is poignant because spoiled fruit had potential for being good, much like the use of the mouth and tongue. These were meant for good use, but become unpalatable when the word is spoiled. Paul urged that we work on producing good words "for edification according to the need of the moment." This is a timely word to edify, which means to build another person up. Notice that the purpose of such speech is to provide grace, which is enablement. Our words are that powerful!

1. How do you define "good"? Do you consider your mouth and hands as instruments of good?

2. Why do we steal? How can we help people by working with our hands?

3. How can our words build other people up and give them grace?

FIVE

Maintaining God's Presence in Your Life

Ephesians 4:30–32 NASB *Do not grieve the Holy Spirit of God, by whom you were sealed for the day of redemption.* *³¹Let all bitterness and wrath and anger and clamor and slander be put away from you, along with all malice.* *³²Be kind to one another, tender-hearted, forgiving each other, just as God in Christ also has forgiven you.*

Understanding the Word. We are privileged to have the Holy Spirit take up residence within us. Remember: we are permeable and meant to be filled with God's presence to enjoy fellowship with him. Although this might sound creepy, it is not; when God is within a person, he does not take over. We are not dominated or obliterated. We retain our identities and are simply enabled to live differently, but not as robots. This divine possession is much different from the demonic possession that is in the Gospels, where we see certain individuals taken over by an evil spirit; that spirit oppresses the person, dominates him or her. It is my view that such may occur when people are very deeply traumatized such that the trauma persists and becomes a controlling force in their life. I would not pretend to understand it completely; nor would I deny that there is a real spirit behind it. However, my main point is that God does not work that way within us; we actually gain our freedom and strength by his grace and retain our own self-control. What this means, however, is that we can resist God even after he has taken up residence within us. When we do so, we "grieve the Holy Spirit of God." This is not a good thing. This is what Paul commanded against in 4:30; after all, the Holy Spirit officially marks us as belonging to God. God has paid our ransom; we belong to him, and one day we will receive new bodies (see 1 Corinthians 6:18–20; Romans 8:22–23).

A helpful booklet I have discovered is titled *My Heart—Christ's Home.*[2] In brief, this little booklet offers a story that compares Christ coming into your life with a person inviting Christ into his or her home as a guest. It begins

---

2. Robert Boyd Munger, *My Heart—Christ's Home* (Downers Grove, IL: InterVarsity Press, 1986).

with Christ standing in the entryway; how much farther do we let him in? It would be rude to leave him standing there. And as it happens, Jesus also kindly wants a tour of your entire house: the TV room, the kitchen, the study, even the closet and attic, which contain painful hidden things. Christ is still a guest; we can refuse him, but he is also a lovingly persistent guest for our own good. The Holy Spirit brings Christ's presence to us and is working for our final redemption.

In 4:31, Paul addressed a vital matter: bitterness and anger. Bitterness is resentment, or re-sentiment, that is, feeling again the hurt of some wrong done to you. Paul gave a list that itemized each element with an "and." Why? He wanted to describe the escalation that can occur when bitterness is not checked; it grows into wrath and anger and keeps stewing; then it manifests in clamor, which is shouting at the person who has wronged you; then it boils over into slander, which is bad-mouthing the person to other people; and finally, it results in "all malice." Real ugly! Paul effectively described an inner-to-outward movement here. He was saying, "Get rid of them all, wherever in the process you may find yourself; it will only escalate!"

When one is tempted to bitterness, what is the antidote? What is one to do? Paul answered this in 4:32 quite directly by providing a list of actions: (1) aim for kindness for one another; (2) be tender-hearted (literally, "good hearted"); and finally (3) forgive each other just as God in Christ has forgiven you. God provides us the example of how to forgive when wronged. An important subtlety in the Greek text lies behind "each other"; this pronoun is actually better translated "yourselves." Forgiving yourselves. This can often be the hardest; if God can forgive you, you can forgive yourself.

1. How have you grieved God's Spirit? What room(s) in your house is Christ wanting to go into?

2. Are you nurturing any anger or resentment that you need to get rid of? Is it escalating?

3. How does God provide a way out of hanging on to our hurts?

WEEK EIGHT

GATHERING DISCUSSION OUTLINE

A. Open session in prayer.

B. View video for this week's readings.

C. What general impressions and thoughts do you have after considering the video, readings, and the daily writings on these Scriptures?

D. Discuss questions based on the daily readings.

    1. **KEY OBSERVATION**: Sin costs us more than we know. Paul really emphasized this by affirming it in the Lord. People who live apart from God encounter all sorts of problems and are lacking many things. Their reference point for life is quite limited, resulting in a focus on their own senses and a quest to gratify themselves. Paul called the Gentile believers to not live like this any longer.

    DISCUSSION QUESTION: What are some of the more striking things that Paul said about living apart from God?

    2. **KEY OBSERVATION**: Believers should not return to their sinful ways as if because of them they found Christ. Rather, believers should learn Christ and be his followers. Paul directed people to the historical Jesus as we have recorded in the Gospels. Jesus is our example, and as his disciples, we follow him. Paul indicated that the believers were taught the truth in Jesus, and this teaching involves a three-step process of transformation in Christ.

    DISCUSSION QUESTION: What is God's three-step process of transformation in Christ? Where are you in the process?

3. **KEY OBSERVATION**: Because believers are members of the same body of Christ, we have an obligation to put aside all falsehood and relate truthfully with one another. Truthfulness is a key hallmark of God's restored people. Also, believers need to carefully watch their anger; it should not lead to sinning and should be dealt with the same day. Otherwise, we give a place to the devil where he does not belong.

   DISCUSSION QUESTION: How important is truthfulness? How do we fail to be truthful to one another?

4. **KEY OBSERVATION**: Humans are made for good, to do good and to give grace to people, especially those in need. Two parts of our bodies are particularly important in this regard: our hands and our mouths. We use these constantly, but for what end? Paul urged believers to use our mouths and hands as agents of good and grace for those around us, particularly for those in need.

   DISCUSSION QUESTION: How do you define "good"? Do you consider your mouth and hands as instruments of good?

5. **KEY OBSERVATION**: The Holy Spirit resides within us for our own good. Yet, we can grieve the Spirit by refusing to live rightly. Perhaps an underlying issue is unresolved bitterness and anger. Such will escalate into fighting, speaking evil, and being filled with malice. The good news is, however, that God has provided a way out in Christ, and he helps us to be kind and good-hearted as well as to forgive ourselves.

   DISCUSSION QUESTION: How have you grieved God's Spirit? What room(s) in your house is Christ wanting to go into?

E. What facts and information presented in the commentary portion of the lesson help you understand the weekly Scripture?

F. Close session with prayer.

WEEK NINE

Ephesians 5:1–14

Imitation of God in Christ in Sacrificial Love

INTRODUCTION

Paul has been instructing believers in how to walk/live in the world in five sections. The central section is 5:1–7, and it is central for a reason: Paul called all believers to imitate God. Specifically, he called believers to walk/live in love by following Christ's sacrificial love. At the same time, Paul continued to explain that certain ways of acting and speaking are off-limits. People will be excluded from the kingdom of Christ and God in the future.

The fourth walking/living section is 5:8–14. Here Paul continued to dissuade believers from close partnership and fellowship with unbelievers and their evil actions through the metaphor of light and darkness. However, believers will shed light into the darkness; it's not as if believers pull themselves away completely; however, they need to have a certain view of themselves and the hoped-for outcome of their being in the world. This is bringing the light of Christ to shine on people's lives such that they are converted to Christ. So, 5:14 ends with this wonderful vision of Christ raising someone up from the dead and shining upon his or her life.

ONE

Imitate God in Love

Ephesians 5:1–2 ESV *Therefore be imitators of God, as beloved children. ²And walk in love, as Christ loved us and gave himself up for us, a fragrant offering and sacrifice to God.*

Understanding the Word. The heart of Paul's exhortation is found in 5:1–2. Nowhere else in Scripture did Paul so directly call believers to be like God, although it is implied in many places. After all, humans are made in God's image; we are like him and are to put on the new self, created like God (see 4:24). Paul elsewhere called believers to imitate him; in 1 Corinthians 4:16 he called believers to "be imitators of me"; then again in 1 Corinthians 11:1, "Be imitators of me, as I am of Christ." Paul also directed the first believers to follow the examples of their leaders (see Philippians 3:17; 4:9; 1 Thessalonians 1:6; 2 Thessalonians 3:9). However, here, in Ephesians, Paul called on believers to be like God. How is this even possible? In what way did Paul mean this? This vision of imitating God is important enough to look at through the lens of Scripture. Where else are believers called to be like God?

In the Old Testament, the people of God were commanded many times, "Be holy, for I am holy" (see Leviticus 11:44–45; 19:2; 20:7), meaning to be set apart for God and unpolluted by what could make one unclean. The Israelites took this call very seriously at times, and radically pulled away from the sinful nations around them; yet, their history as recorded in Scripture is not very compelling; they failed to live into this holiness; we would have fared the same (in fact, all people would have). In the New Testament, Peter quoted this same command to be holy in 1 Peter 1:16 in the thesis statement for his letter; the call to holiness is that important to come directly into the New Testament. However, in Peter's writing we see that being made holy and set apart is for the purpose of fervently loving one another (see 1 Peter 1:22).

Turning to the Gospels, we see that Jesus called his followers to be "perfect, as your heavenly Father is perfect" (Matt. 5:48 ESV); in this context, Jesus particularly had in mind loving all people, even one's enemies. The word "perfect" often gives people some considerable pause—that's impossible! However, this same word "perfect" means "completeness" and "maturity" when referring to people. In Ephesians 4:13 Paul described Jesus as the "mature man" (NASB; literally, "the perfect man") that the church is to grow up into. Paul also described believers as "mature" (1 Cor. 2:6; 14:20 NASB; Col. 1:28), which is their goal (see also Hebrews 5:14 and James 3:2). In the Gospel of Luke, a very similar saying is found: "Be merciful, just as your Father is merciful" (6:36). Again, this is in the context of loving one's enemies (see Luke 6:35).

In Ephesians 5:1, we can also see that the command to imitate God pertains especially to love and mercy, since 5:1 builds on 4:32, which speaks of kindness, compassion, and forgiving ourselves as God has forgiven us in Christ Jesus. Also, in 5:2 Paul continued his admonition to live/walk as Jesus, who loved us, had walked. So, Paul here has opened up our God folders and has asked us to photocopy the contents on God's forgiving love and put it into our own life's folders. This is a large task! We are called to step out, take risks, and even be wronged, and then to forgive in response. We are made for love, and we can do it in Christ. Jesus is the one who showed us how to love in this way, especially our enemies. God does not ask us to do what he himself has not already done. God has given us the resources to love. How? By first loving us. Notice that Paul called believers "beloved children." This brief phrase provides both the basis and the reason for Paul's command to imitate God and love as Christ loved: we are loved first.

1. Is it possible to imitate God? How does Scripture give testimony to this expectation?

2. Is perfection possible for people?

3. In what ways are we to imitate God? What is the example and basis for this command?

TWO

Don't Play with Gods

Ephesians 5:3–4 ESV *But sexual immorality and all impurity or covetousness must not even be named among you, as is proper among saints. ⁴Let there be no filthiness nor foolish talk nor crude joking, which are out of place, but instead let there be thanksgiving.*

Understanding the Word. Paul shifted gears rather quickly in 5:3–4. Why did he move from commanding us to imitate God, walking in love and Christ's sacrifice, to then addressing "sexual immorality and all impurity or covetousness," vices connected to our bodies? This seems quite odd until you remember the God folder. For unbelievers and those who followed after the gods, their gods folder was populated with corrupt gods who were rather humanlike in the worst ways. The gods were personified sources of power that reflected the breadth of humanity, including its best and more often its worst attributes. Rather than humans being made in God's image, as affirmed by God in Genesis 1:27, the gods were made in people's images.

Too often, the gods reflected sexual perversions; pagan cult and sacrifice did at times involve prostitution and sacred sex. The fertility and virility of one's enterprises (business, farming, athletic contests, etc.) may depend on one's imitating the gods in cultic practices. For example, consider father Zeus, hailed the "All-father." He was the worst sexual predator and offender: in Greek mythology, although married to Hera, Zeus was constantly having affairs with more than sixty goddesses and human women, seducing them behind Hera's back (often to meet her wrath) and producing dozens of offspring. Knowledge of Zeus was widespread; he was worshiped twice as much as other gods. When King Antiochus Epiphanes IV captured the Jewish temple in 168 BC, he rededicated it to Zeus Olympus and filled the temple "with debauchery and reveling by the Gentiles, who dallied with prostitutes and had intercourse with women within the sacred precincts, and besides brought in things for sacrifice that were unfit" (2 Macc. 6:4).

This propensity for associating a god with immorality and lewd practices explains why Paul suddenly shifted to forbid sexuality, uncleanness, and greed in Ephesians 5:3. However, Paul discussed sexual immorality in many of his writings, often giving it first place in lists of vices (things to avoid). This sin involves any inappropriate sexual activity: sex before marriage, adultery, and sexual intercourse with a prostitute. Further treatment is provided in the next day's devotion. The other two things to avoid are "all impurity or covetousness"; both are related to sexual immorality. For example, impurity is found listed with sexual immorality in 1 Thessalonians 4:3, 7; Galatians 5:19; and 2 Corinthians 12:21. It refers to the defilement that comes by participating in pagan cultic activities. Finally, in 5:3 covetousness, or greed, may refer to

the lusting after that which does not belong to you; people ⟨
by appealing to the gods. Religion was a mask for greed
sexual immorality, impurity, and covetousness—should not l
believers by outsiders when identifying common Christia
behavior; they are off-limits for believers.

But Paul was not done with vices. In 5:4 he treated vices of the mouth:
filthiness, foolish talk, and coarse joking. This type of talk is contagious.
Having held jobs in various settings, I have seen how pervasive and toxic such
coarse, sexual joking can be; it's easy to say nothing and laugh along with the
others. Instead of such talk, believers are to partake in thanksgiving; this is the
antidote to all these vices—receiving what God has given in thanks and being
content.

1. What sinful behaviors do people justify because of what is or isn't in
   one's gods/God folder?

2. Why did Paul shift from discussing being imitators of God and loving
   as Christ loved to these vices in 5:3–4?

3. How is thanksgiving the antidote to sexual immorality, greed, crude
   joking, and foolish talk?

THREE

Consequences of Living Wrongly

Ephesians 5:5–7 ESV *For you may be sure of this, that everyone who is sexually
immoral or impure, or who is covetous (that is, an idolater), has no inheritance
in the kingdom of Christ and God. ⁶Let no one deceive you with empty words, for
because of these things the wrath of God comes upon the sons of disobedience.
⁷Therefore do not become partners with them;*

Understanding the Word. Paul just got his Big Bertha golf club out. He teed
up 5:5 in two ways. First, he stressed "knowing," which is not translated by
the ESV: "Know for certain this by knowing that . . ." Second, 5:5 supports his
previous commands not to participate in sexual immorality and the other vices.
Why should believers not participate? Quite simply because "everyone who is

xually immoral or impure, or who is covetous [that is, an idolater] has no inheritance in the kingdom of Christ and God." These people are cut off from the inheritance that God wants to give them. This seems severe! Well, we need to understand that God is holy and wants his people to be holy and blameless (see Ephesians 1:4). At the same time, we need to understand that Paul used nouns to describe those excluded in 5:5—these people banned from inheriting Christ's kingdom have become identified with their sin; these sins have so taken over their lives that they become named by the sin. How does this happen? By repeat offending; remember that sin always wants to dominate you. It wants to take over your life. It promises more than it delivers and it wants full control of your life such that it possesses you. Sin is the original identity theft.

Paul addressed sexual immorality in his writings; it is often first in lists of behaviors and attitudes to avoid. In a parallel list in Colossians 3:5, sexual immorality is at the top. The list of vices from the flesh found in Galatians 5:19–22 begins with it; these vices contrast with the fruit of the Spirit in Galatians 5:22–23. In 1 Corinthians 5:1–5, Paul confronted sexual immorality among the Corinthian believers; he concluded his passionate argument by simply commanding them, "Flee from sexual immorality" (1 Cor. 6:18 ESV). Why? Because we have been bought with a price (Christ's sacrifice) and our bodies now belong to God and we should glorify God with our bodies (see 1 Corinthians 6:19–20). In 1 Thessalonians 4:3 Paul defined what God's will is (we should pay attention): "For this is the will of God, your sanctification; *that is*, that you abstain from sexual immorality" (NASB). Also, the first apostles of Jesus, when deciding how to accept Gentile believers into the fellowship of Christ, sent out a letter prohibiting four activities associated with pagan cults; the second item listed is sexual immorality (see Acts 15:19–20). So, one can see that sexual immorality was an issue back then, as it is today. Why is this so?

The Evil One works overtime to trip us up in this area because our identities as male and female, gendered and sexual people, are linked to God's image (see again Genesis 1:27). People yearn for divine connection, but then use that which is God-given in the wrong way. The Evil One attacks us at the place of our divine identity and connection. He tempted Jesus at his point of identity ("If you are the Son of God, do these things . . ."). We are constantly bombarded with images (advertisements, movies, and TV shows) that tempt us. Our sexual desires run deep. These God-created desires, however, need to be used in ways that honor God, our bodies, and each other. The Evil One attacks us at our very best and special part of ourselves; he wants to take that and pervert it. Fortunately, God is in the business of forgiveness; there is no sin that is outside of God's saving work and ability to restore. So, there is no need to get stuck and wallow in our sin. It is a lie to believe you must stay there. Remember that Paul earlier argued, "you did not learn Christ in this [sinful] way" (Eph. 4:20 NASB).

1. How is sin the original identity theft?

2. How often and in what ways did Paul discuss sexual immorality?

3. How special are our gendered identities as male and female? How are these attacked today?

FOUR

Walk as Children of Light

Ephesians 5:8–10 ESV *for at one time you were darkness, but now you are light in the Lord. Walk as children of light ⁹(for the fruit of light is found in all that is good and right and true), ¹⁰and try to discern what is pleasing to the Lord.*

Understanding the Word. Paul made a transition here in Ephesians to move into the next walking/living section that is built around this contrast between the light and darkness. He commanded, "Walk as children of light." Now that God has redeemed us and saved us, it is quite natural and right for us to live in the light. There is freedom here; no more being prey to the darkness; no more shameful sinning; no more hiding; no more fear of God's judgment. Light is a great place to be. Light and darkness is a very old and pervasive metaphor for goodness and badness. We understand what this means quite easily and from an early age. Bad things happen in the dark; evil lurks there. Why? Because evil doesn't want to be seen; it hides in the darkness and wants to take people into that place of darkness, where there is sin, hurt, shame, and hiding. In contrast, the light is the place of clarity, openness, and honesty. It is the place where goodness abounds. As Paul explained, "the fruit of light is found in all that is good and right and true." Remember that the "truth is in Jesus" (Eph. 4:21).

Paul admitted, "at one time you were darkness." This was our starting point, where we had been, all of us. Do you remember that time? It is never a good time: regret, shame, disappointment, frustration, and loneliness. Instead of being in the darkness, believers now have been reborn "as children of light." If God is light, and we are reborn through accepting Christ and trusting in him, then we enter into the light and are children of light. That is why we are "light in the Lord." We have a special task of illuminating the world, bringing light into it. As Jesus said to his followers, "You are the light of the world . . . let your light shine before people, so that they can see your good deeds and give honor to your Father in heaven" (Matt. 5:14, 16 NET). Light consists of good works. Humans were made to walk in the light; we are meant to be good. That is why it feels good to do good. It brings a deep joy. It is right, and it sheds light in the midst of darkness. Our goodness, too, serves the purpose of bringing others into the light so that they also may glorify God the Father. Our light in the world helps others become followers. Although all people struggle with sin, they also have a sense of right and wrong, even if that sense is badly warped. Our bringing light to them actually begins to help restore their consciences, to recalibrate their sense of right and wrong. It is convicting. This is the special task of the Spirit, but that work is seen in our own lives and is contagious. Once they experience the light, they may seek for more; it is that good! They begin searching for God because of the light they see in us.

Paul also urged believers to "try to discern what is pleasing to the Lord." This idea of pleasing the Lord is quite an important one and is found in other places in Paul's writings to describe what believers should do (see Romans 12:1–2; 2 Corinthians 5:9). In this regard, importantly, believers can discern what is pleasing to God; it is goodness, to be sure, but this goodness will be manifested in specific ways that only each person can discern for the benefit of those around us. God will use us as we discern what good to do in order to bring others into the light. When all is dark, it only takes a little light to brighten things up. Shine on!

1. What is the meaning of darkness and light? Why did Paul use these contrasting realities?

2. How does one come into the light?

3. What implications come with being children of light?

FIVE

Bring Light into the Darkness

Ephesians 5:11–14 ESV *Take no part in the unfruitful works of darkness, but instead expose them. ¹²For it is shameful even to speak of the things that they do in secret. ¹³But when anything is exposed by the light, it becomes visible, ¹⁴for anything that becomes visible is light. Therefore it says, "Awake, O sleeper, and arise from the dead, and Christ will shine on you."*

Understanding the Word. We like being productive; the question is, productive to what ends? Unfortunately, people may not reflect on this question much at all. We each have our own reference point. What guides our evaluation of fruitfulness?

Paul once again urged believers not to engage in sinful behavior, here called works of darkness. Such works are pointless. Furthermore, they are unfruitful and unproductive; they don't amount to much. We don't like that! We just need to have the right perspective, God's perspective on what is worth doing. So, rather than being involved with what is not fruitful, Paul urged believers to "[expose] the unfruitful works of darkness." What does expose mean? How do we do this? Our lifestyle and value system that reflects the light will expose the darkness that people participate in. Additionally, Paul chose this word "expose" carefully; it is a technical term that could also be translated as refute in the sense of providing a sustained argument against an opposing viewpoint. In the ancient Greek world, educators wrote books on how to refute arguments. Believers may need to prayerfully consider taking a more vocal stance at times to expose and refute dark deeds. Notice that this is not refuting people, but the deeds themselves, the teachings. Earlier in Ephesians, Paul described that people were carried along by "every wind of doctrine, by people's trickery," which is teaching (4:14). To counter this, Paul indicated that we need to speak the truth in love (see 4:15); we should not be bombastic about this, as sometimes happens when Christians carry signs calling people names. This is not helpful. Rather, Paul illustrated in 5:12 one way to dissuade people from sinful behavior: by indicating that such secretive behavior is "shameful"—it produces a sense of shame in people. When you expose what it does, it gets people thinking. This may produce an internal conviction to change.

If we were to bring this into our own situation today, I believe this refuting would involve informed discussion of the consequences of this or that sinful hurtful behavior. To take just one example, consider the harmful effects of abortion that studies have revealed. Although touted as a women's rights issue, abortion is a women's health issue. Women who have abortions have an increased chance of cancer, reduced chances of subsequent pregnancy, and a high incidence of subsequent depression. Studies show this. Believers need to be informed about the consequences of hurtful sinful behavior. Such refutation, however, needs to be presented in compassionate ways, certainly. We don't expose by pointing a wagging, condemning finger, but by lovingly presenting the truth, caring for the people involved.

In 5:13–14, Paul described how light, when pervading the darkness in people, leads them to Christ, the Light: "anything that becomes visible is light." Paul quoted from several parts of the prophet Isaiah's vision of dead people awakened and having Christ shine on them. They are converted. Although we were once "dead" in our sins, God was merciful and saved us (2:1, 4–7). So too, here, Paul explained, dead people who allow the light to shine in them are awakened and can have Christ shining on them. They become believers, and the light continues to shine in them.

1. How do you determine what is fruitful or not in your life?

2. What did Paul mean by exposing the unfruitful deeds of darkness? How do we do this?

3. How did Christ come to shine in your life?

WEEK NINE

GATHERING DISCUSSION OUTLINE

A. Open session in prayer.

B. View video for this week's readings.

C. What general impressions and thoughts do you have after considering the video, readings, and the daily writings on these Scriptures?

D. Discuss questions based on the daily readings.

1. **KEY OBSERVATION**: Paul called believers to imitate God. This seems like an impossible task, yet it is consistently seen in Scripture, even though it is qualified in the New Testament to refer to forgiving love. God demonstrated such a love in Christ for us, and now has asked us to do the same, just as we have been loved.

   DISCUSSION QUESTION: Is it possible to imitate God? How does Scripture give testimony to this expectation?

2. **KEY OBSERVATION**: Paul urged that sexual immorality, filthiness, greed, foolish talk, and crude joking should not be identified with God's people. Such practices were associated with pagan deities that people imitated. However, God's people have every reason to be thankful, which helps us not succumb to sinful behaviors.

   DISCUSSION QUESTION: How is thanksgiving the antidote to sexual immorality, greed, crude joking, and foolish talk?

3. **KEY OBSERVATION**: Paul wanted believers to know with certainty that people who become identified by their sin will not have an inheritance in Christ's kingdom. Such people await God's wrath. Therefore, Paul commanded believers not to be partakers with them in their sinful living, which includes sexual immorality.

   DISCUSSION QUESTION: How special are our gendered identities as male and female? How are these attacked today?

4. **KEY OBSERVATION**: Believers once were in the darkness but now have come into the light by becoming children of light. This light is goodness that enlightens people all around us; it is attractive and invites others to come out of the darkness also. This goodness helps others become children of light, and this pleases the Lord.

   DISCUSSION QUESTION: What implications come with being children of light?

5. **KEY OBSERVATION**: We have a choice to participate in darkness or in the light. Light exposes the unfruitful deeds of darkness. It causes light to come into people's lives, bringing them to Christ. People exposed to Christ are called to rise from the dead and let Christ shine in their life and become followers of Christ.

   DISCUSSION QUESTION: What did Paul mean when he told believers to expose the unfruitful deeds of darkness? How do we do this?

E. What facts and information presented in the commentary portion of the lesson help you understand the weekly Scripture?

F. Close session with prayer.

WEEK TEN

Ephesians 5:15–33

Filled with the Spirit to Praise God and to Submit to One Another

INTRODUCTION

In 5:15 Paul began the last walking/living section that extends from 5:15 to 6:9. This last section treats fundamental relationships within the Greco-Roman household: husband-wife, parent-child, and master-slave. These same relationships were the subject of ancient political thought that dates all the way back to Aristotle (fourth century BC). After Aristotle, others also discussed these foundational relationships. Paul treated these relationships also, although he thoroughly recast them in light of Christ as the Lord. Paul added this very important perspective to these relationships, which are transformed. What Paul said about these relationships challenged the societal norms of his day. Paul shed light on them according to God's divine plan. For more information on these, see the introduction for Week Eleven.

In this week, we will look at 5:15–33. Paul called believers to walk wisely by being filled with God's Spirit. The Holy Spirit assists us to live wisely. The Holy Spirit of God helps us to be holy in all of our relationships. Preeminent among these relationships is marriage itself, the union of husband and wife. This relationship God has privileged over all others in his creative plan to populate the earth. In fact, the husband-wife relationship reflects Christ's relationship with the church. Paul argued that Christ is the Savior of the church body, which is also his bride. That is how close Christ and his church are; believers are the bride of Christ. In the end, God designed the husband-and-wife relationship to reflect Christ's relationship with the church, in which the church submits

109

and reveres Christ just as Christ loves and gives himself for the church. Wives submit to their own husbands (not to others') while husbands love their own wives as their very own bodies.

ONE

Walking Wisely

Ephesians 5:15–17 NASB *Therefore be careful how you walk, not as unwise men but as wise, ¹⁶making the most of your time, because the days are evil. ¹⁷So then do not be foolish, but understand what the will of the Lord is.*

Understanding the Word. Wisdom was broadly sought after in the ancient world. However, I think that too many people don't care for wisdom; we are inundated with knowledge, lots of it. Knowledge may be quite trivial; it may lead to understanding. However, wisdom is applied knowledge with insight for living in the world. In Paul's day, philosophers espoused ways of living and attracted followers who gained, in turn, wisdom from them. This was a competitive field; which philosophical school should one follow?

Paul boldly entered into this world as he proclaimed the good news of Christ. While preaching at Athens, he was asked by the Stoic and Epicurean philosophers (the two leading schools of thought) to come and present to them his way of thinking (see Acts 17:18); they thought that Paul was preaching two divinities, Jesus and the resurrection. They were half correct, since he proclaimed Jesus as Lord. While preaching the gospel at Ephesus for two years, Paul would lecture at the hall of Tyrannus during the lunch and early afternoon hours (see Acts 19:9–10). Paul called people to carefully investigate their lives, in order to walk wisely.

One of the primary ways of living wisely is "making the most of your time." Paul used a verb here that literally means "buying the time." Time, like money, is a limited resource; it is spent on things. With money, we are often very careful with how to spend it. We value our money and we usually want the most value for it. But do we consider what our time is worth spending on? Although not everyone has the same amount of money, we are each given time. Even though we don't know how much time we have, it is a precious commodity. It is worth a lot. Therefore, we should be careful how we spend it. This is especially true given the fact that "the days are evil." There are lots of temptations and ways to waste our time (and money).

Paul, then, framed this issue of spending time by appealing to wisdom and urging believers not to be foolish. Who wants to be foolish? I don't. Instead of being foolish, Paul urged us to "understand what the will of the Lord is." Well, that seems quite unfair! That is a big topic. Who can claim to know God's will? Well, Paul did. Remember that Paul disclosed God's will, God's plan, several times earlier in Ephesians. By appealing to knowing God's will, he expected the audience of Ephesians to recall those earlier portions of his epistle. In 3:3–4 Paul explained that he was writing down God's mystery now disclosed, and that the Ephesians could read this again as needed. He appealed to what he had written down. He committed it to writing for their benefit. This plan, God's will, is to unify Gentiles and Jews into one body through Jesus Christ (see 3:6). In 1:4–14 Paul explained this same goal in even broader terms: Christ is fulfilling God's purposes as the gospel is proclaimed and believed among the Jews and the Gentiles (1:10–14; see also 2:11–22). So, we can understand that God's will is to reach all people with the gospel of Christ. Our living wisely depends on us understanding that God wants to use us to reach others. This is a good use of our time. In Colossians 4:5–6, Paul made this abundantly clear: "Conduct yourselves wisely toward outsiders, making the most of the time. Let your speech always be gracious, seasoned with salt, so that you may know how you ought to answer everyone." God's will is to extend grace to others, leading them to Christ.

1. How concerned are you about living wisely? How do you define wisdom?

2. How do you spend your time? Is it worth the expense?

3. What is the Lord's will?

TWO

Filled with God's Spirit

Ephesians 5:18–21 NASB *And do not get drunk with wine, for that is dissipation, but be filled with the Spirit, [19]speaking to one another in psalms and hymns and spiritual songs, singing and making melody with your heart to the Lord;*

²⁰always giving thanks for all things in the name of our Lord Jesus Christ to God, even the Father; ²¹and be subject to one another in the fear of Christ.

Understanding the Word. A major form of entertainment in antiquity was banqueting and getting drunk. Dancers might also attend these parties, with whom then the guests could have sex. All this was done in the name of the god of wine, revelry, and theater, Dionysus (in Greek, Bacchus). This divinity was sometimes depicted in a drunken parade with a flute player named Silenus and a train of aroused satyrs (goat-men divinities) and maenads (crazed, drunken women). One's family or business acquaintances might have invited you to a wine party held either at a home or a temple with a drink offering for the god Dionysus—what would you do? Would you risk offending friend or family by not attending?

Paul addressed similar issues in 1 Corinthians 8–10. Here in Ephesians, Paul addressed the matter from the perspective of not participating in sexual immorality and impurity and coarse talk (see 5:3–6) and not getting drunk with wine (see 5:18). Getting drunk, argued Paul, is "dissipation." This is a word that we don't commonly use. What does it mean? The underlying Greek word means "wastefulness" as in "a waste (of time)." If we were to apply this to today, more broadly understanding that wine parties were a major form of entertainment, then we should consider what entertainments of ours are wasting our time.

Rather than getting drunk and wasting time, Paul commanded believers to be filled with the Spirit. This is a rather odd command—how do we let the Spirit fill us? First, we must understand that God wants to fill us, and Paul had prayed for this for the believers (see again 3:19). Second, we play a role here by allowing the Spirit to fill us. We do so by being receptive to the Spirit and placing ourselves in the right posture and activities—hearing and reading the Word of God, praying, meeting with believers, attending worship, and partaking of the Lord's Table (Communion).

What is very important to see here in 5:19–21 is that Paul explained what being filled in the Spirit looks like by providing a list of responses. The list is not comprehensive, but it is representative of the main responses and behaviors that reflect the kinds of things that one who is filled with the Spirit does. Paul explained these responses and behaviors as (1) speaking to one another with spiritual hymns, psalms, and songs; (2) singing and (3) making melody in the heart to the Lord; (4) always giving thanks to God in the name of Christ; and (5) submitting to one another in reverence to Christ. Notice that the NASB translates this last attribute as another command. It is not; it is the last item of the list. How do we submit to one another in Christ? Well, through respecting the giftedness and respective roles that we each have in Christ to serve, love, and relate to one another. So, if I am a teacher, then I submit to my students by preparing as best I can for their learning; they, in turn, submit to learning from me in appropriate and responsive ways. We could talk about other relationships where mutual submission reflects being filled with the Spirit. This is something the Spirit helps us do; it may not be easy, but we do it in reverence for Christ. Critically, Paul in 5:22–33 will describe this mutual submission in terms of the husband-and-wife relationship.

1. What are common entertainments today? What entertainments do you engage in that waste your time?

2. How do you allow yourself to be filled with the Holy Spirit?

3. What does being filled with the Spirit look like?

THREE

Wives and Husbands Are like Christ and the Church

Ephesians 5:22–24 NASB *Wives,* be subject *to your own husbands, as to the Lord.* [23]*For the husband is the head of the wife, as Christ also is the head of the church, He Himself being the Savior of the body.* [24]*But as the church is subject to Christ, so also the wives* ought to be *to their husbands in everything.*

Understanding the Word. Bible translations will often place a subject heading before 5:21 or 5:22. Check your Bible. These headings may be helpful at times, but at other times misleading. The latter is true in this case. Also, as you look at your own Bible, notice how the NASB translation places "*be* *subject*" in italics: this alerts readers that the words are implied from the surrounding context. What this means is that the wife's *submission* to her own husband is implied from Paul's previous statement that, when filled with the Spirit, we submit to one another. This is quite a radical statement, because there is some real sense that husbands submit to their own wives as their wives submit to them. Paul was using the culturally appropriate language (a wife was to submit to her husband in Greek culture), but he was very strategic in providing a larger framework in which a wife's submission occurs: being filled with the Spirit and submitting to one another.

Notice also that Paul did not command the husband to make his wife submit; the submission (which is mutual) is what the wife does, just as also the husband does for his own wife. As we will see in Day Four, the husband submits to his wife by loving her as he would love his own body (this was a countercultural statement!). But in 5:22–24, Paul wanted to provide a second framework for the wife's submission to her own husband: it is analogous to the Christ-and-church relationship. Christ is the head (or origin) of the church, just as the church is Christ's body. In fact, of these two relationships, the Christ-church relationship is more foundational, more fundamental. In God's design for creating the world, he foreknew that humans would fall in sin against him; so he preplanned to send Jesus as the Christ to form a holy body of believers who would be saved. Then, in God's created order, he made humans as male and female, each equally bearing God's image. But before this, God planned for the Christ-church relationship, which is then more fundamental (see Ephesians 1:4–6). So, the husband-wife relationship is really modeled after the Christ-church relationship.

Now, how does Christ relate to the church? He is the head of the body and its Savior. Both of these are political titles. *Savior* was particularly relevant when it came to describing what political and military leaders do for people; they save them. Christ is such a ruler; he saves and delivers. What we learn from Jesus and the Gospels, however, is that the battle looks different from what most people envisioned it to be. Rather than being a military victory and delivering/saving a people from calamity and defeat, the Gospels and Jesus reveal that the real enemy is a spiritual entity organizing other entities against right belief and trust in God. Hence, believers do not take up arms to fight others; we do not fight for land or territory, since our territory is God's kingdom in heaven and in the future, and the war has already been won; all that remains are battles against evil influences.

The wife, then, in comparison to the church, is to submit to her own husband, and not to other men. Many people will read Scripture as if all women are subject to all men; however, the New Testament does not teach this. If there is submission, it is mutual, a wife in relation to her own husband. This was the cultural norm, which is still the case in many cultures around the world. But notice how in 5:24 Paul did not directly use the verb "to subject"; rather, it is implied once again as *"ought to be"* (italicized in the NASB) from the Christ-church relationship, the more fundamental relationship.

1. What frameworks did Paul provide for understanding husband-wife relationship?

2. What is the relationship between a husband and a wife and between Christ and the church?

3. What is indicated by the NASB translation placing *"be subject"* and *"ought to be"* in italics? Why is this important?

FOUR

Husbands, Love Your Wives as Christ Loved the Church

Ephesians 5:25–30 NASB *Husbands, love your wives, just as Christ also loved the church and gave Himself up for her, ²⁶so that He might sanctify her, having cleansed her by the washing of water with the word, ²⁷that He might present to Himself the church in all her glory, having no spot or wrinkle or any such thing; but that she would be holy and blameless. ²⁸So husbands ought also to love their own wives as their own bodies. He who loves his own wife loves himself; ²⁹for no one ever hated his own flesh, but nourishes and cherishes it, just as Christ also does the church, ³⁰because we are members of His body.*

Understanding the Word. In this discussion of wives and husbands, Paul spent the majority of his time addressing the husbands' relationships to their own wives. Why? Perhaps because husbands needed more attention; often in societies, their roles have been given greater privilege, which is seen across multiple cultures around the world.

Paul continued to describe the proper framework for believers to understand the husband-wife relationship: it is Christ and the church. The husband, then, is to model his own relationship to some great extent as Christ related to the church. How did Christ relate to the church? Well, he loved the church and sacrificed himself for her. That is real love. Christ also did this with a particular purpose in mind: to "sanctify her" (5:26). This is a tremendously important qualification, since men may be tempted to sacrificially love and serve their wives to attain their own ends. Husbands may work to placate or manipulate their wives to then get what they want out of the relationship. Indeed, husbands and wives often have a particular dance with one another to try to get out of the relationship what they really want or need. It goes both ways. These dances have been described as scripts that we are often cast into; they are somewhat predictable based on our upbringing and personalized needs and wants. It often goes back to our families of origin and what was given or denied us in our families and what was modeled for us by our parents or caretakers. We bring this baggage into our married relationships and do dances around each other trying to have our needs met.

Paul, however, wanted a husband to model his relationship with his wife on Christ's love, sacrificial giving, and a goal to help sanctify the wife through the Word of God for presentation to God. Christ is working to make the church holy and blameless, that is, pure and without wrinkle or blemish. You see, believers are going to face God someday, and we will be presented before God. Christ is working with the church so as to prepare the church to be presented before God as glorious, in full splendor and honor. Although husbands are not Christ, they, too, participate in this larger role of helping their wives grow in Christ and to be prepared to face God in the final day of reckoning.

How are husbands to love their own wives? Paul explained this repeatedly in no equivocal terms: they are to love their wives as their own bodies. If husbands love and care for and provide for their own bodies, they should do the same for their wives. I know of a husband who drove nice air-conditioned and well-serviced cars while he had his wife buy an old, unreliable car with no air-conditioning from her daughter. Money was not an issue for him. Is this loving his wife as he loved himself? Love would have provided a reliable, air-conditioned car both for himself and for his wife.

1. Why did Paul spend the majority of this section addressing husbands?

2. How did Christ love the church? To what ends did Christ act for the church?

3. In what ways can husbands show equal love for themselves and their wives?

FIVE

Marriage within God's Plan of Salvation

Ephesians 5:31–33 NASB FOR THIS REASON A MAN SHALL LEAVE HIS FATHER AND MOTHER AND SHALL BE JOINED TO HIS WIFE, AND THE TWO SHALL BECOME ONE FLESH. *[32]This mystery is great; but I am speaking with reference to Christ and the church. [33]Nevertheless, each individual among you also is to love his own wife even as himself, and the wife must see to it that she respects her husband.*

Understanding the Word. In 5:31 Paul quoted directly from Genesis 2:24 to affirm God's intention for marriage. It is a union of a man and a woman. Jesus also quoted the same passage from Genesis when he was asked whether it was all right to divorce, since Moses in the Law said that a man could write a certificate of divorce. However, Jesus responded by stating that divorce was not God's purpose for marriage and that Moses only permitted divorce because of the people's hardness of heart (see Matthew 19:3–8 and Mark 10:2–9). So, what Moses allowed in the Law was not God's original purpose for humans in marriage; rather, it was a concession for a people who resisted God's ways. So Paul agreed with Jesus about God's original purpose for marriage as indicated in Genesis.

Paul next affirmed, "This mystery is great" (5:32). What mystery did Paul have in mind? What does the "this" refer to? Some church traditions will appeal to this verse to say that marriage is a sacrament, meaning that it conveys a special grace. Although I believe that marriage is a means of sanctifying grace, that is, grace to help one grow and mature, Paul clarified his meaning in the next sentence: "I am speaking with reference to Christ and the church." We must remember that earlier in Ephesians, Paul explained that God's mystery now revealed was the formation of Jew and Gentile believers into one unified political body, the church. The Christ-church relationship is the more fundamental relationship upon which the husband-wife relationship is modeled.

It is important to understand that in 5:32–33 Paul concluded his arguments, and thus 5:32 shows the priority that Christ and the church has for believers. Then, in 5:33 Paul concluded his admonitions first for the husbands and then for the wives. The application of what Paul has been advocating boils down to each particular couple. That is why Paul used the phrase "each individual among you." This stressed the responsibility of each husband. Also, this responsibility is restricted once again to "his own wife"; he should not be loving other men's wives. Rather, the husband is to love his own wife as he loves himself. She should be treated with the same dignity and respect and care as he would give himself. What Paul urged here was countercultural for husbands.

Likewise, Paul summarized the wife's relationship to her husband as one of respecting him. Notice that the verb "to submit" or "to subjugate" is not used here. We saw in 5:22 and 5:24 how Paul implied the verb from the surrounding context: first, from 5:21 and the life of being filled with the Spirit such that believers "submit to one another out of reverence for Christ" (NIV), and, second, from the earlier portion of 5:24, where Paul said, "the church is subject to Christ." That Paul did not use the verb "to submit" in the summary conclusion of 5:33 has huge implications for understanding his point. Paul was urging that wives deeply respect their husbands. This word "respect" is the same as that translated "reverence" in 5:21 with respect to one another.

From what I have read, what Paul affirmed of husbands and wives corresponds to our most essential needs. Women especially appreciate being loved and cherished, and the husband should offer this to his bride. Likewise, husbands especially appreciate being respected in the relationship. What Paul urged is that both are possible in Christ when believers are filled with the Spirit.

1. What is God's purpose for marriage?

2. How does 5:32–33 effectively summarize Paul's argument in 5:22–31?

3. What do wives and husbands especially appreciate? How is this possible?

WEEK TEN

GATHERING DISCUSSION OUTLINE

A. Open session in prayer.

B. View video for this week's readings.

C. What general impressions and thoughts do you have after considering the video, readings, and the daily writings on these Scriptures?

D. Discuss questions based on the daily readings.

1. **KEY OBSERVATION**: Believers ought to be concerned with wise living. Paul urged us to spend our time wisely since there is so much evil around us. Rather than squandering our time and being foolish, believers are encouraged to understand what God's will is: to spread the gospel to the nations.

    DISCUSSION QUESTION: How do you spend your time? Is it worth the expense?

2. **KEY OBSERVATION**: It is tempting to fill oneself with entertainments. In antiquity and for people today, getting drunk was a major entertainment. But there are many others. Rather than wasting time, by seeking always to be entertained, Paul urged believers to be filled with the Spirit and provided representative behaviors and attitudes of what this looks like.

    DISCUSSION QUESTION: What does being filled with the Spirit look like?

3. **KEY OBSERVATION**: Building upon the previous description of believers submitting to one another, Paul turned to address wives in relation to their own husbands (but not to other men). However, the husband-wife relationship is patterned after the Christ-church relationship, which is the more fundamental relationship. Moreover, Christ is described as the head and Savior of the church body.

   DISCUSSION QUESTION: What frameworks did Paul provide for understanding the husband-wife relationship?

4. **KEY OBSERVATION**: Husbands are on the hook. Typically, husbands have greater privileges and freedoms in society than wives do. How will husbands reflect Christ's example and purposes to their own wives? Husbands and wives often fall into predictable scripts to try to have their own needs met. However, Paul called husbands to love their wives as themselves and to see their wives as Christ sees the church. Christ works to sanctify the church through the Word of God to present the church holy and blameless to God.

   DISCUSSION QUESTION: Why did Paul spend the majority of this section addressing husbands?

5. **KEY OBSERVATION**: The book of Genesis defines marriage as the union of a husband and a wife. Jesus affirmed this when explaining that divorce was not God's plan for marriage. Paul likewise affirmed Genesis by quoting it in today's passage. However, the great mystery is Christ's relationship with the church, which the husband-wife relationship models. In the end, Paul urged a husband to love his own wife and the wife to deeply respect her husband.

   DISCUSSION QUESTION: What is God's purpose for marriage?

E. What facts and information presented in the commentary portion of the lesson help you understand the weekly Scripture?

F. Close session with prayer.

WEEK ELEVEN

Ephesians 6:1–9

Responsibilities of Parenting and Being a Master

INTRODUCTION

We saw last week that Paul treated the primary relationships of the household—the husband and wife—although this relationship is subordinated to Christ the Savior's relationship to the church body. In 6:1–9, Paul discussed the other two fundamental relationships in the typical household: parents with children and masters with slaves. This rounds out Paul's treatment of the typical household, but Paul thoroughly recast these fundamental relationships in view of Jesus Christ as the Lord and God's salvation plan for humanity. Let me explain a bit further.

Paul explained that the husband-and-wife relationship corresponds to God's purposes in creation. He quoted from Genesis 2:24 to support his view. Next, when treating the parent-child relationship, Paul quoted from the Law and the promise about having long life in the land. Here, education in the Lord is the key. Finally, when treating the master-slave relationship, Paul discussed the final judgment of each person, whether slave or free, before the Lord. So, Paul moved from creation, to the promise of long life now, and finally, to the final judgment before the Lord. Thus, Paul effectively saw the household structure and its relationships to be reflective of the structure of God's relationship with people in the past, present, and future.

ONE

A Key to Long Life

Ephesians 6:1–3 NASB *Children, obey your parents in the Lord, for this is right. ²HONOR YOUR FATHER AND MOTHER (which is the first commandment with a promise), ³SO THAT IT MAY BE WELL WITH YOU, AND THAT YOU MAY LIVE LONG ON THE EARTH.*

Understanding the Word. In this chapter, Paul turned next to address the children in the parent-child relationship. Paul commanded them to obey their parents "in the Lord." This phrase does not modify parents, as if Paul were talking about the person who gave spiritual birth to someone by leading him or her to Christ. Rather, Paul was indicating that the children's relationship with their parents is overseen by and governed by the Lord. The phrase "in the Lord" provides a perspective from which a believing child is to obey his or her parents. At a certain age, a child may need not to obey because the parents are having them do something contrary to the Lord. The child's relationship with the Lord is the primary relationship.

This word "obey" is different from the word "subject" used of the church's response to Christ. Here, obey indicates full compliance. Paul supported this command with the simple statement "for this is right." It is common human understanding that children should obey their parents. This is generally true.

How old are these children? Does this refer to adult children? The Greek language has several different words to refer to children of different ages. This word is the most generic one. However, since Paul was addressing them directly, they must be of reasonable age to comply. Furthermore, Paul earlier quoted from Genesis 2:24, "A MAN SHALL LEAVE HIS FATHER AND MOTHER AND SHALL BE JOINED TO HIS WIFE" (Eph. 5:31 NASB). Full compliance ends at marriage. Using this same principle, full compliance ends when the child moves out. As much as parents may want their independent adult children to be fully compliant, this is not what Paul commanded here in 6:1.

Nevertheless, in 6:2 Paul indicated a continuing principle that children of all ages honor their parents. This sense of honor does not strictly mean to obey, but rather indicates a good esteem or value that one has for one's parents. They brought us into the world, and we ought to provide respect for them at this level. Sadly, sometimes parents can be quite lousy, if not even completely out to lunch and outright hurtful. Some children have been abandoned or abused by their parents. Paul was assuming the best here. Each adult child will need to consider prayerfully how best to show honor to his or her parents; but such honor does not mean full obedience or compliance to them.

Paul quoted from God's Ten Commandments given to Moses (see Exodus 20:12; Deuteronomy 5:16). He added that this command to obey one's parents is the first command with a promise. The promise has two parts to it: "THAT IT MAY BE WELL WITH YOU, AND THAT YOU MAY LIVE LONG ON THE EARTH." In God's creative design, parents were to be a source of provision and blessing for their children until the point of death and even after death through the passing on of an inheritance. Parents are to educate and pass along the most precious traditions to their children. Specifically, parents were to instruct their children in the way of the Lord (see 6:4 in Day Two). Thus, to honor one's parents involves receiving all these benefits from them as God intended. If these things occur, generally it will go well with each of us, and we will live long(er) on the earth.

1. What age of children did Paul address? Does a person ever stop being a child?

2. What does it mean to obey and to honor one's parents?

3. What benefits can parents offer their children in God's design for the family?

T W O

Fatherly Influence

Ephesians 6:4 NASB *Fathers, do not provoke your children to anger, but bring them up in the discipline and instruction of the Lord.*

Understanding the Word. In this verse, Paul turned to address fathers. Why only fathers? Is the word "fathers" also inclusive of mothers? I don't think so, since Paul earlier referred to parents. So, Paul was focusing his admonitions on fathers. Why? Typically, either a mother or a slave (called a tutor) educated the younger children; the older children possibly received more education with a specialized teacher. In Galatians 3:24–25, Paul described a child under a tutor when discussing the role of the Law until Christ came: the Law was like a tutor for us (children) until we came of age as adults and placed our trust in Christ. As Paul continued to develop this analogy, he also explained that children are under managers and guardians until they come of age, and at that time they are full adults eligible to receive an inheritance (see Galatians 4:1–2). Fathers were often not directly involved with the education of their children. However, in the typical family, the fathers led the household in matters of religious devotion. They were like priests.

Paul here described the father's role with two commands. First, he gave a negative command: "do not provoke your children to anger." This prohibition seems rather odd—how does a father provoke his children to anger? I can think of four ways, and there are probably others. The first is through neglect. A father's neglect can have long-term consequences of anger at what he has done. This may take time, but often such neglect is deeply hurtful and painful for adult children. A second way that a father may provoke his children to anger is through over-involvement and micromanaging. A third way a father may provoke his children to anger is through having unrealistic and unsupportive high expectations. It is possible for fathers to expect such great and specific things for his children so as to place lots of pressure on a son or a daughter, which can create anger. The father may be well-intentioned in his desire for his children to carry on the family business, tradition, or name, but will create frustration in his children. For a son, such an expectation may be quite crippling into adulthood, especially if the father shows little esteem or support for the son. Finally, a father may provoke anger through showing favoritism among his children. Favoritism values one child over another. Scripture contains several examples of such hurtful favoritism; this was also seen in the culture of Jesus' and Paul's day. It is still common. So, whether through neglect, micromanagement, unsupportive high expectations, or favoritism, a father must work not to provoke his children to anger.

Paul's second command is positive: "bring them up in the discipline and instruction of the Lord." What is distinctive here is education about the Lord. Although others will educate children in various subjects, it is the father's role to educate about the Lord. This is quite important since fathers were considered the priests of the family. They led the family to worship the traditional gods, deceased family members, and other local deities. But for Paul, there is only one God and one Lord, Jesus Christ. Paul called on fathers to represent Christ and educate their children in the Lord. In this regard, the two words that Paul used are quite significant. The first word, "discipline," is the Greek word *paideia*, from which we get the word *pedagogy*; paideia refers to a comprehensive education. In antiquity, whole treatises were written on paideia in general or of a special individual (e.g., the *Cyropaedia*, or "The Education of Cyrus," by Xenophon in the fourth century BC). The second word, "instruction," particularly has to do with correction and teaching what to avoid. In matters of believing in the Lord Jesus, the father plays an instrumental role guiding and correcting his children.

1. What are ways that a father may provoke his children to anger?

2. In Paul's view, what is a father's role in raising his children? What is a father's responsibility?

3. How does a father bring up his children in the discipline and instruction of the Lord?

THREE

Slaves of Christ

Ephesians 6:5 NASB *Slaves, be obedient to those who are your masters according to the flesh, with fear and trembling, in the sincerity of your heart, as to Christ . . .*

Understanding the Word. In 6:5–9, Paul addressed the last relationship found within many households: the master-slave relationship. He dignified slaves by speaking to them directly in this passage. Paul reframed their obedience "as to Christ." Slavery was common: "As many as one-third of the population of the empire were enslaved, and an additional large percentage had been slaves earlier in their lives."[3] Slaves were inherited or acquired from

---

3. S. S. Bartchy, "Slave, Slavery," in *Dictionary of the Later New Testament and Its Developments*, eds. Ralph P. Martin and Peter H. Davids (Downers Grove, IL: InterVarsity Press, 1997), 1098.

purchasing captives from war, by buying existing slaves, or from slaves having children thus born into slavery. Most important for a slave was who owned him or her. Highly educated slaves were greatly valued, especially in the urban areas. Slaves could be freed by their masters, or, they could work their own businesses, earning money and then purchasing their freedom. Some slaves preferred to keep working for a family. Freed slaves adopted the name of their owner; among the most prestigious freed slaves were those from the imperial family, "those of Caesar's household" as mentioned in Philippians 4:22 (NASB), who often continued working for their master, sometimes in a quite high capacity, like the Roman procurator (governor representative) of Judea, Felix, a freed slave of the Emperor Claudius, whom Paul met (see Acts 24:22–27).

At first glance in Ephesians, it might appear that Paul had betrayed slaves by presumably maintaining the status quo—why would Paul not command the masters to free their slaves outright? Well, not every slave wanted this, and not every slave was capable of sustaining himself or herself. Some were considered like family and even after their freedom continued to serve faithfully. In his letter to Philemon and the house church, Paul strongly urged Philemon (the master) to free his slave, Onesimus, for Paul's sake. However, this was a close friend of Paul's, and there were extenuating circumstances. Ephesians, however, was a circular letter reaching people more broadly and speaking to quite a variety of circumstances.

It is helpful to understand that Paul offered a more nuanced view of slavery in 1 Corinthians 7:21–23: "Were you called while a slave? Do not worry about it; but if you are able also to become free, rather do that. For he who was called in the Lord while a slave, is the Lord's freedman; likewise he who was called while free, is Christ's slave. You were bought with a price; do not become slaves of men" (NASB). We can see that he discouraged one from becoming a slave and urged slaves to become free, if they were able, by earning money by working business on the side; but this possibility was not available for every slave. Some slaves were in terrible situations, but for them to flee or try to escape would only have brought punishment or even death. Paul urged slaves to consider themselves Christ's freedmen—that is, those who take on the name of Christ and live in honor and devotion to their (former) master. So, when reading Paul's commands here to slaves, we should assume that they understood that he was not advocating for them to stay as slaves, but if possible, to earn their freedom. This later possibility is suggested by how Paul ended his appeal to them, by mentioning being "free" (Eph. 6:8). Paul was providing a broad framework for situations where the slave may not have been working for a master who was a believer in Christ and was not yet free, or worse yet, had no chance to become free. What was a slave to do in that very common situation? Paul was very specific, and in Day Four's devotion, we will look at Paul's admonitions. In today's reading, though Paul made clear that Christ was the slave's true Master.

1. What is your understanding of slavery?

2. Did Paul betray slaves by issuing commands to them?

3. Across Paul's letters, what instructions and hope did Paul offer to slaves?

FOUR

Rendering Service as to the Lord

Ephesians 6:6–8 NASB *not by way of eyeservice, as men-pleasers, but as slaves of Christ, doing the will of God from the heart. ⁷With good will render service, as to the Lord, and not to men, ⁸knowing that whatever good thing each one does, this he will receive back from the Lord, whether slave or free.*

Understanding the Word. In Day Three, we looked at the broader institution of slavery in the Mediterranean world. It would be wrong to over-generalize; practices and circumstances varied. Roman practices varied from earlier Greek ones. Both were different from more recent and modern forms of slavery, as occurred in the American, British, Dutch, and other colonies and in the current sex trade. Paul was not writing to address these atrocities. It is also significant that the New Testament writers, including especially Paul, introduced themselves as "slaves" (see the NLT's translations of Romans 1:1; Philippians 1:1; Titus 1:1; and James 1:1). Paul argued also that believers are "enslaved to God" (Rom. 6:22), and more than this, we have been adopted as God's children, who have an inheritance (see Romans 8:21; Galatians 4:7). For Paul to identify himself as a slave was not meant to diminish the heartache that existed for many slaves, but rather communicated an understanding of the plight of many as well as to communicate the freedom that was given to believers by Christ, who is their heavenly Master: they were in relationship and obligated to give honor and faithfully serve Christ.

Within our American society, which has no legal slavery, the closest analogy for applying Paul's commands to slaves and masters is the working environment. Much of what Paul said has immediate application to the work environment. So let's review Paul's commands to slaves.

First, in 6:5 Paul clarified that such earthly masters are only so in the "flesh"; there is a Master "in heaven" above the earthly master. Paul reminded the masters of this in 6:9. Second, Paul urged the slaves to obey them "with fear and trembling." Why? Because masters had full authority over their slaves, even over death. Third, such fear and trembling were qualified further with the phrase "in the sincerity of your heart, as to Christ." This speaks to the inner motivation and ultimate devotion of the slave: Christ owned them. Fourth, Paul urged that slaves not simply do things to please people or out of "eyeservice"—that is, to appear better. Fifth, rather, Paul reminded slaves that they belong to Christ; therefore, they should do "the will of God from the heart." Remember that the will of God is that all people would be saved (see 1 Timothy 2:4). Paul was calling slaves to see their position from the perspective of God's desire to win people over; obedient and sincerely serving slaves may very well win over their masters to the Lord.

Sixth, Paul reminded them for whom they were working—the Lord—and so urged such service to be given with "good will." This term addresses one's attitude and means "favor, benevolence, affection, good attitude." Finally, Paul urged slaves to understand that God accounts for the good that we do and will reward us on that basis. Such rewards are not the basis of our salvation, but reflect the reality of standing before God to give an account of what we have done for him after receiving Christ. What we do matters not simply now, to bless and to win people over to God's love in Christ, but in our futures. God watches us and cares how we do things, how we work and spend our time. We will receive back according to what we have done—all of us, regardless of our station, "whether slave or free." That Paul ended his admonition to the slaves on this note laid before them the equality that exists with God. God is impartial. Also, slaves may have opportunity to gain their freedom, but still will be accountable to God in Christ.

1. Why would New Testament authors identify themselves as slaves?

2. In what situations today do Paul's admonitions to slaves have the most relevance?

3. Within Paul's admonition to slaves, which ideas and perspectives are most pertinent today?

FIVE

The Impartial Master in Heaven

Ephesians 6:9 NASB *And masters, do the same things to them, and give up threatening, knowing that both their Master and yours is in heaven, and there is no partiality with Him.*

Understanding the Word. Paul turned in this verse to address the masters' role in their relationship with their slaves. As much as we would have wanted Paul to tell masters to free their slaves, it was not as easy as this, since many slaves would not have a means to provide for themselves and would have to sell themselves again into slavery. Rather, Paul's strategy was to change the way masters viewed their slaves and treated them. Paul's approach actually was a better one, since he addressed matters of the heart. In the long run, masters, if they complied with Paul's admonition, would radically change the institution of slavery by their treatment of slaves, from the inside out. We need to look carefully at Paul's wording here, which is quite powerful in the underlying Greek.

Paul commanded masters to "do the same things to them." What?! That's right, *the same things.* The Greek text stresses this by placing "the same things" first in the sentence and also by explicitly marking the recipients of the same things: "to them." So, the list of seven things that Paul had just commanded the slaves to do in 6:5–8 were to be taken up by their own masters. The masters must see themselves as rendering service as to Christ in the sincerity of their hearts; they must see themselves as not doing things by way of eyeservice (as men-pleasers), but as slaves of Christ. Masters should be doing the will of God from the heart, which means seeking to win people to God in Christ. Masters should be rendering service with good will as to the Lord, and not to men. And masters should know that whatever good thing they did, they would receive back from the Lord. Thus, the masters' whole view of their relationship to their slaves was transformed and placed within the purview of God in Christ. What this meant is that they should not be treating their slaves as other masters treated their slaves, and thus maintaining the status quo. Their treatment should be noticeably different and humanizing; they were to bring dignity to the relationship. Truly Paul was showing how life in the Holy Spirit should result in mutual submission to one another (see again 5:21); here slave to master and master to slave.

In addition to doing the same things to their slaves as Paul urged the slaves to do for their masters, Paul commanded the masters to "give up threatening." This word used here for "threatening" referred to "boastful promises" most fundamentally, as well as to "threats." English translations consistently translate it in terms of threats. It is not hard to imagine how commonly masters might boast about their possessions, which included slaves, and make promises that involved the (improper) use of their slaves. Slaves were objects for the use of one's guests. Likewise, threatening slaves conveyed one's power over them; one would also have to follow through with the punishment. To not carry through with a threat would be dishonorable and was unthinkable. So, Paul nipped the situation in the bud, so to speak. He addressed the initial movement and inertia toward the abuse of power and hurting the slaves, which was the masters' prerogative rightfully under the law. However, not everything lawful is right; *not everything that we have a "right" to do is right to do.* Masters had the full authority over their slaves and could do whatever they wished with them. However, Paul declined this possibility. He disavowed masters of their right to abuse their slaves. The perspective that Paul especially wanted the masters to understand was that they and their slaves shared the same Master in heaven, Christ the Lord. The Greek text is particularly poignant at communicating this by adding the word "both" and conjoining "their . . . and yours." Christ is an impartial Master.

1. How specifically did Paul change the master-slave relationship from the inside out?

2. What are "the same things" that Paul commanded the masters to do?

3. How does a proper view of God in Christ change the master-slave relationship?

WEEK ELEVEN

GATHERING DISCUSSION OUTLINE

A. Open session in prayer.

B. View video for this week's readings.

C. What general impressions and thoughts do you have after considering the video, readings, and the daily writings on these Scriptures?

D. Discuss questions based on the daily readings.

1. **KEY OBSERVATION**: In the Lord, children should obey their parents. One of the Ten Commandments was that they should honor them, which comes with two promises: that it would go well with them and that they would have long life on the earth.

   DISCUSSION QUESTION: What does it mean to obey and to honor one's parents?

2. **KEY OBSERVATION**: Fathers played a minor role in the direct education of their children. However, each functioned as a priest within the family. Paul commanded fathers not to provoke their children to anger, but rather, to provide a comprehensive education in the Lord Jesus that also involved correction.

   DISCUSSION QUESTION: In Paul's view, what was a father's role in raising his children? What was a father's responsibility?

3. **KEY OBSERVATION**: Paul addressed the next relationship within the household by speaking to the slaves. Slavery was quite common in

antiquity, and Paul addressed individuals caught up within the institution. Paul urged them to see themselves as offering service to Christ, their heavenly Master.

DISCUSSION QUESTION: Across Paul's letters, what instructions and hope would Paul offer to slaves?

4. **KEY OBSERVATION**: Paul helped slaves to view their service as a means of accomplishing God's will, which is to save all people. Thus, as Paul gave directions for slaves, he addressed matters of their motivation and the future reward they would receive for doing whatever good thing each one had done.

   DISCUSSION QUESTION: Within Paul's admonition to slaves, which ideas and perspectives are most pertinent today?

5. **KEY OBSERVATION**: Paul commanded the masters to treat their slaves the same as those slaves were to treat their masters. By so commanding, Paul changed the relationship. In fact, Paul wanted the earthly masters to know that they too had a Master, in heaven, who is impartial.

   DISCUSSION QUESTION: How does a proper view of God in Christ change the master-slave relationship?

E. What facts and information presented in the commentary portion of the lesson help you understand the weekly Scripture?

F. Close session with prayer.

WEEK TWELVE

Ephesians 6:10–24

Arrayed in the Battle Armor of God for Witness in the World

INTRODUCTION

The climax of Ephesians is found in 6:10–20. This is followed by the epistolary conclusion that rounds out the letter in 6:21–24 by discussing Paul's circumstances and offering a benediction of peace, love with faith, and grace from God the Father and the Lord Jesus Christ. Paul again wanted the Ephesian believers' God folders to be appropriately filled.

The climax of Ephesians arrests our attention by describing the nature of the Christian struggle and God's armor offered to us. Indeed, believers in Christ are engaged in a battle even though God in Christ has already won the war. There are still hostile agents against which we as believers must take a stand. In God's plan, however, we have been granted the right and honor to don God's own messianic armor. This armor is tried-and-true; Jesus wore it, and now we wear it too.

ONE

Mighty and Powerful against All Evil Forces

Ephesians 6:10–12 NASB *Finally, be strong in the Lord and in the strength of His might. ¹¹Put on the full armor of God, so that you will be able to stand firm against the schemes of the devil. ¹²For our struggle is not against flesh and blood,* *but against the rulers, against the powers, against the world forces of this darkness, against the spiritual* forces *of wickedness in the heavenly* places.

Understanding the Word. Paul signaled that he was wrapping up his epistle by using the word "Finally." He offered the command to "be strong in the Lord and in the strength of His might." Three power words are used here. Throughout Ephesians, Paul indicated that believers are well-connected to the ultimate source of power, Jesus, who is seated at God's right hand of power, "far above all rule and authority and power and dominion, and every name that is named, not only in this age but also in the one to come" (1:19–21 NASB). Believers are seated with Christ, and their futures are secure (see 2:6–7). There is no doubt or question about that. Paul himself received God's grace and power inside to carry out God's work for him (see 3:7). In fact, such grace and empowerment has been given to each and every believer according to Christ's gift; he won the victory and freed us as captives to serve within the church body (see 4:7–16).

Paul explained more about God's provision of power by describing it using the powerful metaphor of armor, specifically Roman armor. People across the Roman Empire saw repeatedly such armor on soldiers and then on statues and other monuments celebrating Rome's powerful defeat of its enemies. Engraved on ancient coffins or memorials for deceased soldiers, one can find all six pieces of armor that Paul listed here and that will be discussed in the next several days.

But why is such armor needed at all? Well, there are several layers to answering this question. First, God has so determined to work within and to save people by allowing them to work their way through the mess of this world themselves engaging in the struggle. God has not just beamed us up and away or removed the evil from the world quite yet. Instead, in God's wisdom, to effect maximum salvation of humans, he asks us to learn to resist evil from inside the system. God entered the system himself in the form of his Son, Jesus, the Jewish Messiah and King, who walked among us and faced the same sorts of temptations that we face—and overcame the Evil One! We are now called to use the same manner and methods to follow after Jesus—that is, to experience both suffering and God's deliverance—as we live in this world, doing God's will.

Second, we need the armor of God because we face spiritual opposition in a close, hand-to-hand combat or struggle, a word that referred originally to wrestling. God's supply of armor matches the schemes of the enemy. We cannot be better equipped. One dictum of war is to know your enemy. Our enemy is named as the devil, who has "schemes." This Greek word is *methodos* (literally, "methods") and was used earlier in 4:14 to describe deceitful human scheming that keeps people like infants carried around by every wind of teaching. That's the devil's work: to keep humans from reaching their potential as mature people made in God's image. So, corresponding with human deceitful schemes, the devil uses a host of entities, beginning with human rulers, then progressively higher tiers of entities that were taught in the pagan culture to be behind and above human rulers: the powers (gods and goddesses), the world forces (the planets and stars), and every other spiritual force captures anything else. Believers struggle against any named force laying claim to our devotion and fear in the place of God.

1. What power has God made available to believers? How is it made available?

2. What is the nature of our struggle? What are the schemes of the devil?

3. What forces of evil call for our devotion in the place of God?

T W O

God's Messianic Armor, Part I

Ephesians 6:13–14 NASB *Therefore, take up the full armor of God, so that you will be able to resist in the evil day, and having done everything, to stand firm.* *¹⁴Stand firm therefore,* HAVING GIRDED YOUR LOINS WITH TRUTH, *and* HAVING PUT ON THE BREASTPLATE OF RIGHTEOUSNESS, . . .

Understanding the Word. After Paul named the entities of the first believers' struggle in their original pagan context, he repeated the command to put on the full armor of God. The stated purpose for this is to be able to resist when the evil day comes. Paul emphasized this point by adding "and having done everything, to stand firm." What Paul was communicating is that the evil day, the (really) bad days, will come to believers. We must be ready. They happen to everyone and can discourage us terribly. We have an enemy that is active in the world to resist God working in us. As uncomfortable as this may be, the threat is real; the temptations are real. In Luke's Gospel, we learn that in addition to the initial set of temptations that Jesus faced from the devil at the start of his ministry (see Luke 4:1–13), he had other trials and temptations (see 22:28). Also, Jesus told the parable of the sower who sows the Word of God, and some of the seed fails to produce fruit in people because they succumb to temptation (see 8:13). Then too, in the prayer that Jesus taught believers to pray, the final two requests are "and lead us not into temptation, but deliver us from the evil one" (Matt. 6:13 NIV). Our enemy is real, and the temptations are too.

Standing firm is what Paul called us to do. So important is this idea militarily that the Roman statesman Cicero in his Laws for the ideal governing state (*Legibus* II.xi, 27–28) described the benefit of setting up a cult to a god of "Standing Firm." We as believers are in a standing army of God in a struggle that affects each one of us. To help us stand firm, God supplies armor. The capitalized statements in 6:14–15 indicate that Paul was quoting from the Old Testament. (He also did this in 6:17.) In fact, Paul has woven together statements from several different portions of Isaiah's vision of God's armor to describe the anticipated Jewish Messiah (see Isaiah 11:5; 52:7; 59:17). Isaiah and Paul were using this imagery to explain something deeper about the nature of the battle: the physical armor pieces are the vehicles to explain the profound importance of divine attributes, virtues, and spiritual entities. Paul did this in other places in his writings, but never so completely as here (see Romans 13:12; 2 Corinthians 6:7; 10:4; 1 Thessalonians 5:8). However, rather than conceiving of the enemy and the nature of the battle in human militaristic terms (that is, merely in terms of "flesh and blood"), Paul conceived the warfare in terms of truth, virtue, and God's attributes, including God's Word. In fact, compared to Isaiah, Paul emphasized even more such armor by describing God's armor as being like Roman armor in its completeness.

He began with a reference to girding up our loins with truth. Truth, remember, is what the people of God are to embody. Paul urged believers to speak truthfully in love to one another (see 4:15, 25) because the truth is in Jesus (see 4:21) and we are created to be like God in the holiness and righteousness that comes from the truth (see 4:24). The starting point of our struggle against the devil is the truth about our condition, our sin, and about what God says to save us. When tempted, I have experienced victory by knowing the truth about the sin and where it would take me. Sin deceives and keeps us in the dark, away from the truth of the light. The next piece of armor is "the breastplate of righteousness" which guards your vital organs, especially the heart. By righteousness, Paul had in mind rightly living or living righteously; the term that is often translated as "righteousness" was a core virtue in antiquity and concerns justice and rightly relating to one another. In the gospel, Christ sets the standard: he reveals God's righteousness to us.

1. How would you describe temptation? How often does it come to you, and how do you resist?

2. Why is it important that the believers' armor is God-given, tried, and true?

3. How important are truth and righteousness for God's people? Why are these foundational?

THREE

God's Messianic Armor, Part II

Ephesians 6:15–17 NASB *and having shod* YOUR FEET WITH THE PREPARATION OF THE GOSPEL OF PEACE; *[16]in addition to all, taking up the shield of faith with which you will be able to extinguish all the flaming arrows of the evil one. [17]And take* THE HELMET OF SALVATION, *and the sword of the Spirit, which is the word of God.*

Understanding the Word. The next armor piece addressed is the appropriate footgear, here "THE GOSPEL OF PEACE." Our feet take us places; they direct us and leave an imprint. Paul envisioned movement of the gospel as he depicted the gospel of Christ in relation to our feet, which move us about. It is particularly important for us to understand that Christ's gospel is the announcement of a victory, the victory over sin, death, and the devil. The word "gospel" was also being used of the reign of the Roman emperors. Augustus's ruling was called "the good news" (the same term), just as also the Romans proclaimed the *Pax Romana* and the *Pax Augusta*, the Roman and Augustan Peace. In response to military campaigns in Hispania and Gaul, the Romans erected the Altar of Augustan Peace (*Ara Pacis Augustae*) to honor the goddess of peace (*Pax*) for the peace that Augustus had achieved: the monument in Rome shows images of the abundance of the divine favor and the peace achieved by the Romans. Paul argued instead that Jesus himself is our Peace (see 2:14). Jesus unified the warring parties (Jews and Gentiles) into one new humanity, the body of Christ. Just as the Roman army advanced its peace through military conquest, so in God's chosen way believers are to advance the gospel of peace of Christ.

After footwear, the soldier takes up the shield of faith. In Paul's description, he added more details to describe the enemy's weapons for which the shield was effective: flaming arrows. The Roman shields could be formed with an exterior covering that could be soaked with water to better stave off the fiery arrows. Certainly such fiery arrows were well-known, but they were not always used; regular arrows were common. We should consider why Paul made explicit mention of these fiery arrows. At this time, two possibilities are possible. The first is that the god Zeus/Jupiter was known for these fiery arrows (lightning strikes) and the lightning bolt was sometimes depicted with him as arrows. Other deities shot arrows also (e.g., Artemis, Apollo, Cupid). A second consideration is quite similar in that the god of love, Cupid, shot fiery arrows of lust. In philosophical discussion mention is often made of the fiery dart of sexual passion. In either case, Paul would be then indicating that evil forces (as then conceived as personified divinities) could launch attacks that are rebuffed by our shield of faith, or faithfulness. The word for faith can mean both trust in and faithfulness toward the object or person of that trust. In the case of a fiery dart of lustful passion, one's faithfulness to God and one's spouse would stave off all the attacks.

The next piece of armor is the helmet of salvation. Paul probably intended us to think about the mind as the source of thought in relation to God's salvation. Throughout Ephesians, Paul stressed the importance of knowledge and prayed for the believers to be enlightened with knowledge. The type of knowledge has to do with God's salvation, which included our deliverance out of the darkness into the light. It is vital for believers to remember God's salvation graciously granted in Christ.

Finally, Paul described the Word of God as the sword of the Spirit. The Holy Spirit inspired the writing of God's Word, and proper enlightenment from Scripture is enabled by God's Spirit. The Word of God is an offensive weapon; however, we need to wield it carefully (like any weapon) and non-offensively.

1. How is the gospel of the peace of Christ like and unlike the Roman Peace (*Pax Romana*)?

2. What does the shield of faith ward off? How?

3. What is likely signified by the helmet of salvation? How is the sword of the Spirit, the Word of God, an offensive weapon?

F O U R

Paul Is Christ's Ambassador in Chains

Ephesians 6:18–20 NASB *With all prayer and petition pray at all times in the Spirit, and with this in view, be on the alert with all perseverance and petition for all the saints, [19]and pray on my behalf, that utterance may be given to me in the opening of my mouth, to make known with boldness the mystery of the gospel, [20]for which I am an ambassador in chains; that in proclaiming it I may speak boldly, as I ought to speak.*

Understanding the Word. Following on the heels of the describing God's armor, Paul turned next to address prayer, which one might consider the proper breathing of a soldier. Prayer is the air environment, the necessary breathing, of a soldier. Also, just as every Roman soldier would placate and pray to and sacrifice to his divinities, so Paul called believers to pray "at all times in the Spirit." Paul emphasized such prayer by urging that "all prayer and petition" be made "at all times." Praying is as constant as the breathing that keeps us alive. Prayer is our ongoing relationship of speaking and listening to God. Prayer is precious.

Just what believers are to be praying for is "all the saints." Believers around the globe are to be lifting one another up constantly. In fact, Paul used the verb "be alert," which may indicate that peril exists; otherwise, the rather unique verb means "to be attentive, concerned about, care for." Such praying is not easy and requires discipline and focus. In fact, Paul qualified his command by adding "with all perseverance." This phrase communicates something of the endurance needed to maintain this kind of praying. There is great benefit for us in praying like this, because it allows us to see the world from God's vantage point. We learn about the spread of the gospel of peace; we learn about the world's terrible struggles and plights. Even as I write this, just two days ago, terrorist attackers with guns and bombs killed forty-one people and injured more than a hundred at the very part of the airport that I walked through just fourteen hours later. Our world is a troubled one and needs prayer.

Paul also asked for believers to be praying on his behalf that he would proclaim the gospel of Christ with boldness. It is not selfish to ask for prayer; as we learn more and more about God's will and participate in outreach and service that builds up the body of believers, we too should be asking others to pray for us. The work of the spread of the gospel through apostles, evangelists, through church plants, and through our shining good deeds and refuting the deeds of darkness is certainly worthy of our asking others to pray for us. We each play an important role.

Paul in particular was imprisoned, probably at Caesarea Maritima, and was meeting periodically with various governing officials. He was "an ambassador in chains." Paul understood that he belonged to a different political system and program, to Christ's way of being in the world. Although Paul did make appeal to his citizenship, either as a Jew or a Roman citizen, he preferred not to do this but rather to suffer shame for Christ's sake. However, as a Roman citizen, he did have some rights, specifically, to a fair trial and proper treatment. It was a fine line for him to know when to speak up and say, "I'm a Roman citizen." It stopped the beatings immediately (such was not allowed for someone accused; a person must be tried first and found guilty). Eventually, he would have to appeal to Caesar Nero, and would be sent there. Whether Paul knew of that yet or not, it doesn't matter so much for us except to know that Paul was facing the same type of human rulers with whom we struggle. Satan often works through them, and our struggle involves attempting to win them over. Paul elsewhere asked believers to pray for kings and governing authorities (see 1 Timothy 2:1–4) so that believers could live peaceably as our witness to them that God wants to save all people.

1. How often do you pray? Is it realistic to think of prayer as breathing?

2. How often do you ask for prayer? How might this be helpful for you and others?

3. What did it mean for Paul to call himself "an ambassador in chains"?

FIVE

Incorruptible

Ephesians 6:21–24 NASB *But that you also may know about my circumstances, how I am doing, Tychicus, the beloved brother and faithful minister in the Lord, will make everything known to you. ²²I have sent him to you for this very purpose, so that you may know about us, and that he may comfort your hearts. ²³Peace be to the brethren, and love with faith, from God the Father and the Lord Jesus Christ. ²⁴Grace be with all those who love our Lord Jesus Christ with incorruptible love.*

Understanding the Word. At the end of Paul's letters, it is not uncommon to find a description of his travel itinerary and other logistical details. We observe this in 6:21–22. Paul was a political prisoner for Christ, and believers who had come to faith because of his ministry in Asia Minor wanted to know about his welfare, what was the latest news. While Paul preached the gospel at Ephesus, Luke reported that "all who lived in Asia heard the word of the Lord, both Jews and Greeks" (Acts 19:10 NASB). So Paul sent Tychicus to comfort their hearts by relating to them about his circumstances.

Who was Tychicus, and what was he doing? First, Paul gave him a rather full description as "the beloved brother and faithful minister in the Lord." The reason for this is that Tychicus was being more formerly introduced to the believers who would receive Ephesians as someone that Paul would later be sending to them. Tychicus would follow the letters that Paul would send first; this strategy would allow for two opportunities for people to learn about Paul—the first through reading Ephesians (we don't know who carried it), and the second through the subsequent visit of Tychicus. Paul used this strategy on other occasions, as seen in Titus 3:12: "When I send Artemas or Tychicus to you, make every effort to come to me at Nicopolis, for I have decided to spend the winter there" (NASB). Second, Tychicus was a ministry companion of Paul's that he relied upon on many occasions (see Colossians 4:7; 2 Timothy 4:12). So important was Tychicus that he helped bring the portion of the collection from Asia Minor (see Acts 20:4). What a blessing it is to have someone like Tychicus! What a blessing to be someone like Tychicus! We learn from Paul's letters that Paul had forty named ministry companions in various capacities.

Interestingly, one-quarter of these were women. Paul was a networker; he understood the benefits of relationships and working together in community. This didn't come easily; nor did Paul always see eye to eye with people, like when Barnabas and he got into a sharp dispute over whether to bring Mark on a missionary journey since Mark had earlier bailed out on the previous one (see Acts 15:39).

At the very end of Ephesians, Paul concluded with a benediction in which he offered peace for the brethren and love with faith from God the Father and the Lord Jesus Christ. Then he offered grace to those who love the Lord Jesus. Paul summarized important themes that appear across the letter; he also concluded with the God folder open. Christ is our peace; God has shown us love; believers are to have faith in God in Christ through the Spirit; grace comes from God and the Spirit through our Lord Jesus Christ.

In an important final thought, Paul added a phrase translated in today's passage as "with incorruptible *love*." However, the word "love" is not in the original Greek text (that is why it is placed in italics in the NASB); translated literally, the last statement is "in/with incorruptibility." The term "incorruptibility" more normally is used by Paul to refer to "human immortality of everlasting life" (see 1 Corinthians 15:42, 50, 53–54). It appears, then, that Paul concluded by making reference to the grace that will be given to believers having been raised with Christ in the ages to come (see Ephesians 2:4–7).

1. When and why does Paul send Tychicus?

2. Do you value social networks of fellow workers? How important are these relationships for the gospel of Christ?

3. With what important final note(s) does Paul end Ephesians? Why would he end this way?

WEEK TWELVE

GATHERING DISCUSSION OUTLINE

A. Open session in prayer.

B. View video for this week's readings.

C. What general impressions and thoughts do you have after considering the video, readings, and the daily writings on these Scriptures?

D. Discuss questions based on the daily readings.

> **1. KEY OBSERVATION**: Paul called believers to be strong with power and to don God's armor. We have an enemy in the devil, who uses progressively higher levels of entities as schemes against us: human rulers, powers, and so on. Such entities call for our devotion and fear, but we must stand against them and worship only God.
>
> **DISCUSSION QUESTION**: What is the nature of our struggle? What are the schemes of the devil?

> **2. KEY OBSERVATION**: Believers are to stand firm in the evil days that will come. Temptations abound, but believers have God's armor available for them to wear. The first item listed is the belt of truth, covering our loins. The second is the breastplate of righteousness, which refers to rightly relating to one another and protects our hearts and the core of our being.
>
> **DISCUSSION QUESTION**: Why is it important that the believers' armor is God-given, tried, and true?

3. **KEY OBSERVATION**: Paul further described the armor of God as including the gospel of peace with which our feet are to be shod; the shield of faith; the helmet of salvation; and the sword of the Spirit, which is the Word of God. Each piece of armor plays a vital role in the battle against evil influences.

   DISCUSSION QUESTION: How is the gospel of the peace of Christ like and unlike the Roman Peace (*Pax Romana*)?

4. **KEY OBSERVATION**: Paul pleaded for believers to pray at all times for the saints, and for him. It is not wrong to ask people to pray for you. We need to do so, as we each contribute to God's saving purposes in the world. Paul was representing God's kingdom and considered himself an ambassador for Christ, the Lord. He asked for believers to pray for him to proclaim the gospel with boldness.

   DISCUSSION QUESTION: How often do you ask for prayer? How might this be helpful for you and others?

5. **KEY OBSERVATION**: Paul worked with people and sent Tychicus to relay important information that would comfort believers. He was imprisoned and people wanted to learn about his circumstances. Paul concluded by offering a blessing that summarizes important themes in the letter.

   DISCUSSION QUESTION: With what important final note(s) did Paul end Ephesians? Why would he end this way?

E. What facts and information presented in the commentary portion of the lesson help you understand the weekly Scripture?

F. Close session with prayer.

CPSIA information can be obtained
at www.ICGtesting.com
Printed in the USA
LVHW04n1611180818
587001LV00007B/11/P